Connecting with Students'
WILL TO SUCCEED

The Power of Conation

Cheryl Gholar & Ernestine Riggs

PEARSON

SkyLight

Glenview, Illinois

Connecting with Students' Will to Succeed: The Power of Conation

Published by Pearson Professional Development
1900 E. Lake Ave., Glenview, IL 60025
800–348–4474 or 847–657–7450
Fax 847–486–3183
info@pearsonpd.com
http://www.pearsonpd.com

LCCN 2003112896
ISBN 1-57517-891-5

V

Z Y X W V U T S R Q P O N M L K J I H G F E D C B A
10 09 08 07 06 05 04   15 14 13 12 11 10 9 8 7 6 5 4 3 2

The eagle drew courage from an innate wisdom. Until her children discovered their wings, there was no purpose for their lives. Until they learned how to soar, they would fail to understand the privilege it was to have been born an eagle. The push was the greatest gift she had to offer. It was her supreme act of love. And so one by one she pushed them, and they flew!

—David McNally in *Even Eagles Need a Push*

Dedication

This book is dedicated to the millions of unsung heroes, who day after day, year after year, climb seemingly insurmountable mountains, swim against the currents of mediocrity, race against the winds of defeat to provide emotional and physical support for any child in need. To those who go into battle, armed with love of the human adventure, knowledge of their craft, high expectations and the belief that in spite of any adversity, they can and will make a difference in the lives of children. To those who fight real and imaginary dragons to open new ways of thinking, this book is dedicated.

To those who have an overwhelming commitment to the academic, emotional, and social development of all students, we honor the dedication of your work. To those who understand that the will to commit to the act of teaching moves one beyond intellectual somersaults that separate and divide schools of thought, placing little value on the worth of a child, we applaud you for having no time for "no-win verbal babble." To those who are determined that the gift of knowledge will not slip through a child's grasp, we are humbled. To those who know that the act of teaching begins with faith in one's humanness, and resonates in the innermost lives of others, we are awe-inspired.

Authentic teaching and learning bring us to the deepest reality of our existence if, as teachers, we never lose sight of the human journey, and our ability to be moved by that which is important in life, including something as simple as a child's need to dream. This becomes the first step to attaining knowledge that triumphs over darkness. Authenticity initiates our collective expedition to the domain of conation, and authentic success.

This book celebrates the facilitators of learning who know and actualize, on a daily basis, what it mean . . . to teach.

Contents

CHAPTER 1 — Understanding Conation 7

CHAPTER 2 — Where Learning Lives 33

An Invitation to Learn 61

Captivate, Connect, and Cultivate 93

When in Doubt…Teach 119

Acknowledgments

First, we thank Pearson SkyLight Publishing Company for recognizing the importance of this work and the value of its contribution to education. Their courageous stance is to be commended. We are truly indebted to Stephanie Jackson-Prather and Chris Jaeggi for taking the risk of buying into our belief that the concept of conation can help to make a difference in the lives of our young people.

We are sincerely grateful to our editor, Peggy Kulling, whose insight, ideas, tenacity, thoughtful guidance, and enthusiastic "Think about this" approach kept us moving and stretching the limits while challenging us to reach more deeply into our collective conative spirit.

We are intellectually grateful for current and historical research that validates our hypothesis and findings regarding conation as one critical link of momentous proportion to high performance. We acknowledge all who explore opportunities to transform ordinary classrooms into powerful places of learning. We honor all who demonstrate the academic courage to grow beyond their own and perhaps, others' expectations.

We are also exceedingly grateful to those courageous teachers who added to the authenticity of this book through their personal voices and those of their students. We thank Regina Alexander, Juwana Foster, Rhonda Kimbrough, Monica McClinton-Palmer, Sheryl Myrieckes, Jeannie Pimental, Lynn Rule, and Samantha Sims. We acknowledge the creative skills of Mitch Bejeck, for his years of visually crafting our ideas into colorful and engaging works of art that assisted us in effectively making our presentations meaningful for teachers, parents, and administrators.

And we are most appreciative to Susan Ciucci for her ongoing friendship and guidance and for allowing us to use her as our sounding board.

As individuals first, and authors second, we would be remiss not to pay homage to significant individuals in our personal lives who have been living examples and role models of an unadulterated conative spirit and to those who have been our incomparable cheerleaders and supporters.

I hold in great esteem my parents, Theodore and Geneva, who led gently while inspiring my life with their values of wisdom and truths, which have served me well as I have chosen to serve others as a teacher and counselor. In their awesome reverence of God, they encouraged me to never wait for the sun but to be a light whether alone or in the presence of others. When possible, become an effectual collaborator with those seeking to create a new day.

I acknowledge my children, Tiffany and Christopher, for their accomplishments and struggles to find place and purpose to share their voices in the world. I have learned so much from them—of the resilience and fragility of the human spirit. To my husband, John, whose faith in me has always been my inspiration as well as my reality check. His tireless support during this project has given me the will to confront my own obstacles and stand firmly in my beliefs.

To my sister Moonyueen, whose inner work and inner light taught me the virtue of silence, quiet time, and space for growing, healing, and reinventing myself. To my brother, Nicholas, and his wife, Helen, whose humorous and serious views of life have given me the gift of living purposefully, to dance with the twists and turns in life and laugh out loud at myself and the world when things get too crazy. To my sister Teanna and her husband, Jim, for being there to guide, support, and share their shoulders during times of stress—boosting my ideology of what's possible and providing me with the gift of a wonderful computer, which made this book possible. To my sister Marla and her daughters, Danielle and Jennifer, whose incredible faith under fire took them to places where the faint of heart would never tread or even stand for a moment without faltering. They taught me to release the power of conation in my life.

To my sister Theajyneen and her husband, Claude, for lives that hold no fear of things that can be changed when confronted by faith.

—CHERYL GHOLAR

As an educator who loves learning and awakening the thirst for knowledge in the lives of others, my appreciation for such an awesome gift goes to two of the greatest teachers I will ever know, my parents, Rufus and Catherine, who taught me to love God first, then myself; whose love, perseverance, and belief in my abilities provided me with indelible memories and tools of life, thus equipping me with their principles and wisdom, which serve as a firm foundation on which I have constructed my way of life and my sense of self-determination in matters that make a difference.

To my loving son, Arnold, Jr.; my devoted husband, Arnold, Sr. (may he rest in peace); my sister Margaret Thompson, who has been there for me through the laughter and tears, you are an untiring angel walking on this earth; and Nina Gates, my other mom—all of you are the brightest stars in my universe with your own special brand of the conative spirit. And to four other significant people in my life—Gwendolyn Traylor, Ednarene Smith, Arvon Prentiss, Sr., and Dr. Judy Stewart—thank you for your love, prayers, encouragement, support, and friendship and for just being you! All of you are irreplaceable gifts.

—ERNESTINE RIGGS

Introduction

Living and Learning

Where does the incentive to live, learn, and succeed reside? Growing research indicates that the dimension of its strength lies in an intangible place *within* the learner. Lepper defines *intrinsic motivated learning* as "learning that occurs in a situation in which the most narrowly defined activity from which the learning occurs would be done without any external reward or punishment" (1988). The act of learning and achieving become their own reward. This self-motivation, self-effort, striving, and volition are also referred to as conation.

What students believe about themselves, others, school, and the future shows up with them in school every day. Understanding the integral role of conation in academic achievement demystifies why some students choose to engage in learning and others choose to resist active participation. Encouraging and capturing the *will* to learn is critical to the learning process. The *will* to learn is the foundation upon which learning takes place. The fundamental underpinning of conation is goal-oriented action, action that leads to academic achievement and action guided by ethical principles. The strength of goal-oriented action is in direct alignment with student beliefs.

The conative connection focuses on two behavioral objectives:

1. **Knowing** what one has to do to achieve a specific goal
2. **Doing** what one has to do, intentionally giving one's personal-best to achieve a specific goal

Between knowing and doing are beliefs and paradigms—structures that define who we are as individuals. Beliefs and paradigms are the support systems that govern the direction to the *will*. The strength of one's *will* to touch the lives of students plays a critical role in who will choose to teach in the conative domain. In this paradigm or way of viewing our role as teachers or students' roles as learners, teaching means reaching students where they live. And learning means saying yes, I am willing and available, willing to receive and give my best as I strive to grow. Through understanding the dynamics of this domain, we can help students achieve higher levels of knowing and being (Malloch, 1990). In the process of teaching and learning, the conative domain brings together the power of one's intellectual, emotional, moral, and intuitive strengths to form streams of light, hope, wisdom, and new dimensions.

When various conative techniques and measures are implemented, students are encouraged to flourish and grow in skill, character, and personal determination. Students discover that learning is a task and an experience, a personal experience, often a revelation that opens them to a bigger world within, as well as outside of themselves. Sometimes large and transformative or perhaps small yet insightful, informing the learner of a detail that may have been overlooked or unknown prior to a specific learning opportunity, conation connects the student to personal beliefs about learning a particular concept or topic and the responsibility to do what is expected to learn. In the classroom, it all begins with a relationship. It begins with the *will* to teach on the part of the facilitators (teachers) and the *will* to learn, which falls on the students (see Figure 0.1). This breakthrough factor is *conation*—the *will,* inner strength, determination, and volitional force that drives change. Conation connects one to dreams; it connects one's dreams to the *will*. The *will* becomes bonded to a commitment, and suddenly one finds the inner self working toward a goal. Through the passion of the *will,* one pursues excellence; in the pursuit of excellence, one can live the dream.

Fundamental Framework

The will to teach . . .
> the perseverance and determination on the part of the teacher

The will to learn . . .
> the perseverance and determination on the part of the learner

The will to believe . . .
> the perseverance and determination on the part of the teacher
> and learner

The will to listen and understand . . .
> the perseverance and determination on the part of the teacher
> and learner

The will to strive . . .
> the perseverance and determination on the part of the teacher
> and learner

Figure 0.1

What You'll Find in These Pages

Connecting with Students' Will to Succeed: The Power of Conation provides a fresh look at inner resources that are available to each of us. Perceptions of reality are examined, ways to support and enhance learning are provided through research-based information, activities, quotes, and examples. Behaviors that block learning are explored and solutions are discussed.

In the development of each chapter, thoughtful and reflective consideration was given to determine the content, organization, and format. In addition, current research has been included focusing on various educational principles such as learner-centered approaches, motivational factors on effective teaching and learning, productive teaching and learning environments, and cognitive, affective, psychological, and conative constructs.

Each chapter begins with a student and a teacher voice, acquired from elementary to high school students and from pre-service and practicing teachers who share their thoughts, feelings, beliefs, and philosophies on school, learning, teaching, and life. Each chapter ends with two "Lessons from the Heart of Learning," consisting of instructional strategies and activities that promote the conative approach to teaching and learning. These lessons have been developed for primary, elementary, middle, and high school students.

Chapter 1, "Understanding Conation," provides a research-based definition and explanation of conation.

Chapter 2, "Where Learning Lives," focuses on teaching and learning in the conative domain.

In chapter 3, "An Invitation to Learn," teachers are challenged to reflect on and examine their personal teaching philosophies and their beliefs about and expectations of the students they encounter on a daily basis.

Chapter 4, "Captivate, Connect, and Cultivate," takes the reader on a heroic journey in pursuit of discovering how the "will" or self-effort inspires dynamic and courageous teaching, awakening transformational and intrinsically motivated learning.

The book concludes with chapter 5, "When in Doubt . . . Teach." This chapter boldly challenges teachers to honestly scrutinize, analyze, and reevaluate their paradigm about the purpose of teaching and learning. It encourages teachers to courageously create conative connectivity in relationship to students as learners and teaching that effectively responds to students' needs, gifts, and capabilities.

The choice is ours to integrate the wisdom of conation into the language of learning and our lives. In *The Conative Connection,* Kathy Kolbe observes that "[t]he potential of integrating the conative into education alone staggers the imagination" (1990, p. 3).

When we choose not to teach with conation in mind, we are doing no more than simply tossing out information while observing who will catch it. Yet, in reality, without the will to learn, information often gets caught up in the winds of chatter and verbal babble disconnected from the actual learning process.

Ultimately, this book is meant to encourage and inspire effective, authentic teaching, learning, and success by exploring ways to connect the heart, mind, and *will* of all students and teachers to the mission and promise that each and every student is entitled to the uninhibited pursuit and attainment of learning, and literacy, for life.

Understanding Conation

Student

How do I know I'm successful in my personal life? Well, there's an **inner light that glows so bright,** I can **never see myself giving up.** I can describe my thoughts in one word, **happy!**—FOURTH GRADE STUDENT

Teacher

Once mutual trust is established we move forward to explore exciting possibilities that often have not been tried in reading instruction. **Teachers discover new ways to engage and challenge students to learn. Innovative ideas are always welcome. Our work together is most gratifying,** especially when we see rewarding results! At our school, we are a team. **Teachers share** with each other insights and strategies that are making a difference. **Student involvement and test scores are increasing.** I guess you can say that **staff cohesiveness and accountability is evolving in ways that we are proud of** as a school community.

—ELEMENTARY SCHOOL TEACHER

Where Does the Will to Live, Learn, and Succeed Reside?

Educators have learned that we cannot make students learn. The age-old adage, "You can lead a horse to water, but cannot make it drink," applies aptly to students. We can teach them, attempt to motivate them, but we cannot learn for them. Students must be proactive in order to learn. First, they must possess the *will* to learn; then, they must make an effort and apply their energies to learning tasks.

Teachers cannot *give* students the desire, drive, or will. No teacher, parent, or any other stakeholder has the power to make students learn. *Drive, will,* and *effort* must emanate from the learner. However, teachers can awaken and cultivate these elements through authentic and creative teaching. This is not an impossible expectation, as these factors have been a part of the students' psychological structure since birth. Unfortunately, these elements are often overlooked, underestimated, or misunderstood. Teachers have literally ignored the payoff of these elements as they struggle through each day, trying to coerce students into learning the required subject matter.

Teach from the Heart

Effective, knowledgeable, and empathetic teachers teach from the heart! Teaching that comes from the heart connects with the mind and soul of the learner. Teachers should assume responsibility for creating excitement, enthusiasm, and the will to learn, succeed, and survive in those students who have given up the race long before approaching the starting line.

The concepts of *will, drive,* and *effort* have been ignored too long by too many students. Students often think that learning is not very important in the scheme of things, and, therefore, they see little reason to devote a great deal of time and effort to their learning. It has been noted that at the middle school level, teachers should emphasize mastery and improvement instead of relative ability and social comparison. However, observed and empirical data has demonstrated that teachers do the opposite. Teachers place more prominence on relative ability, competition, and social status and less emphasis on self-motivation, effort, self-improvement, and life-planning strategies. This focus results in a decline in students' ability to perform tasks, a drop in their self-esteem and self-confidence, and, of course, lower academic achievement (Anderman & Midgley, 1996).

We are all teachers. We are all learners, in place called life, with a gift called time.

Growing research indicates that the will to learn lies *within* the learner. The consequences are profound. Does this inner place have a name? Is it intangible and immeasurable? Current research exploring the psychology of learning examines the determinants of learning and how these determinants relate to the learners' willingness to take the initiative and the responsibility for his or her own learning.

What moves us and then makes us move? It is *conation*—the will, inner strength, determination, and volitional force that drives change. Conation connects us to our dreams; it connects our dreams to our *will.* When the *will* commits itself, we suddenly find our inner self working toward a goal. Through the passion of the *will,* we pursue excellence, and in the pursuit of excellence, we can live our dreams.

What Is Conation?

The distinction between volition, intellect, and emotion has been observed throughout the ages by puzzled and mystified scholars. Although the word *conation* has been used for 200 years in psychological literature, it still remains one of the most obscure words in the English language. *Conation,* from the Latin word *conari,* means one's capacity to strive.

German and Scottish scholars in the late eighteenth century described the mind as having three capabilities or faculties: cognition (knowing), affection (valuing people, things, or ideas), and conation (striving and directing one's energy toward a goal). The idea of conation was ignored during the nineteenth and much of the twentieth century, because social scientists became disinterested in things you couldn't see or count. And, who can see something as abstract as the human will?

Huitt (1999) indicates that one reason why research into conation lagged behind research into cognition and emotion is that conation is often intertwined with the cognitive and affective domains and is difficult to separate from them. He explains that both Wechsler's scales of intelligence (Walsh & Betz, 1990) and Goleman's (1995) construct of emotional intelligence include conative components.

Recent research acknowledges that conation is essential to the acquisition of learning. Conation is critical if an individual is to engage in self-direction and self-regulation (Huitt, 1999). Since conation represents the will to act or freedom of choice, it is an essential part of human behavior (Bandura, 1997). The fundamental attributes of conation are:

- belief,
- courage,
- energy,
- commitment,
- conviction, and
- change.

These six attributes describe the fundamental framework of conation and how the act of learning occurs. *Belief* gives us *courage.* Courage inspires our powerful *energy.* Energy sustains our *commitment* to our goal(s). (See Figure 1.1.) When we activate and combine the first four attributes—belief, courage, energy, and commitment—we strengthen our *conviction.* When we purposely act upon our convictions, we experience internal and external *change.*

When we engage these six attributes, the possibilities for learning and making a difference are endless. These qualities must be in place for the teacher and learner to undertake the rigorous journey into the intensity, challenge, and excitement of learning. They provide clarity as to how and why we choose to learn and behave in certain ways.

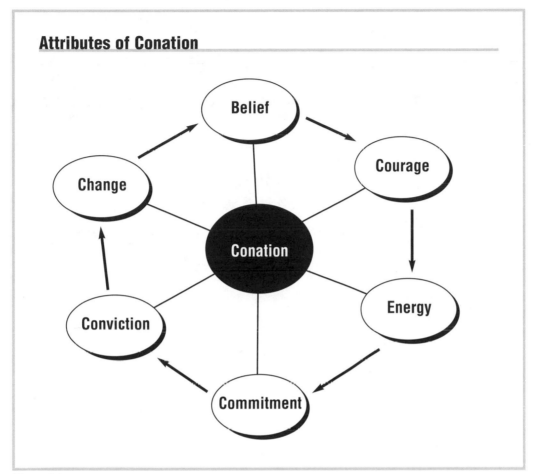

Attributes of Conation

Figure 1.1

Conation in Context

As explained earlier, the mind has historically been divided into three parts—cognition (knowing), affection (feeling), and conation (will). The following paragraphs describe each of the three parts.

The Cognitive Domain

The cognitive domain, or cognition, can be defined as an intellectual process by which one acquires, stores, retrieves, transforms, and uses knowledge. An advanced form of cognition is metacognition. Metacognition occurs when learners are aware of their own cognitive

The Gift of Conation

Conation introduces you to your gifts and to the world around you, releasing you from fear of boundaries and limitations. It allows you to know instinctively that everything is going to be all right. Conation helps you understand that school is a place where you can use your gifts to meet the academic expectations you've set for yourself as well as standards the school has set for you.

processes and know when, where, and how to use these processes to facilitate and support their learning.

Knowledge can be categorized into three basic elements:

1. **Content:** knowing what, where, and when (teaching skills)
2. **Context:** connecting knowledge with a task, environment, or expected outcome (researching skills)
3. **Cognition:** constructing knowledge through perception, reflection, critical thinking, and common sense (learning skills)

The learning process is a multifaceted and complex task that requires the implementation of a variety of diverse techniques. Researchers agree that there is no single approach—no made-to-order, foolproof *modus operandi*—that fully explains and demonstrates how children learn at the cognitive or metacognitive level. The behaviorists, cognitive psychologists, and social cognitive theorists all have their theories; each theory provides a piece of the puzzle, but none describes the ultimate solution.

However, educators globally recognize Piaget's and Vygotsky's research and theories on how children construct knowledge. Piaget (1929) believed children constructed knowledge by assimilating and accommodating their physical and social environment. Vygotsky (1978) espoused that children acquire cognitive processes through guidance and interactions with others in their environs. He firmly believed that children were able to develop independently to a certain level, but had the potential, with the help and guidance of adults or peers, to advance to an even higher level of cognitive development. He called this the zone of proximal development (ZPD), which is the difference between what a child can do independently and what he or she can do with scaffolding or support. ZPD has become the underpinning for effective classroom instruction.

The Affective Domain

Affection can be defined as a feeling or emotion as distinguished from cognition, thought, or action. The affective domain addresses one's feelings, emotions, attitudes, self-perceptions, self-concepts, values, self-esteem, and self-efficacy. Research indicates that the affective domain significantly influences one's ability to learn or perform (Bandura, 1986).

THE Will to Teach

Sowing Seeds of Success

We teachers must focus all of our energy on fertilizing the seeds (our students) and preparing and tilling the soil (promoting learning that renews and transforms itself) if we hope to harvest beautiful, ripe fruit (students who are mentally, emotionally, socially, and intellectually healthy and productive). When teaching and learning are transparent and fluid, students discover that the possibilities of education and life are limitless, students believe in their potential to be the very best that they can be, and students realize that they can become a truly "no limit" person.

The affective domain also plays a pertinent partnership role with conation. Both affection and conation are connected to motivation; affection is connected to extrinsic motivation and conation is connected to intrinsic motivation. Affection plays a role in learning: students' positive or negative reactions and responses to learning goals and performance tasks are, unfortunately, often dependent upon their positive or negative relationships and interactions with peers, parents, and teachers.

The Conative Domain

In *Flow: The Psychology of Optimal Experience* (1990), Csikszentmihalyi describes conation as intrinsic motivation, coming from within. Conation is the inner strength that compels us to reach down to the depth of our will in order to reach a goal or complete a task. This inner strength can be equated to self-actualization in Maslow's (1987) Hierarchy of Needs. However, some theorists explain that "students are most likely to be intrinsically motivated when two conditions exist:

> **Our dreams are only limited by how far our beliefs and actions will take us.**

1. they have high self-efficacy regarding their ability to succeed at classroom tasks, and
2. they have a sense of self-determination—a sense that they have some control over the course that their lives will take" (Ormond, 2000).

Lepper (1988) defines *intrinsic motivated learning* as "learning that occurs in a situation in which the most narrowly defined activity from which the learning occurs would be done without any external reward or punishment." This self-motivation, self-effort, striving, and volition are also referred to as conation.

Figure 1.2 summarizes the facets of the cognitive, affective, conative, and metaconative domains and illustrates the differences and the interconnectedness between each domain.

Teachers can help students, as well as themselves, better understand the role conation plays in learning and how it operates in relationship to the cognitive and affective domains. These domains are interrelated when

Comparing the Cognitive, Affective, Conative, and Metaconative Domains

DOMAIN	ATTRIBUTES	EXAMPLES
Cognitive	Knowledge, intellect, problem solving, critical thinking, reflective thinking, comprehending	I must learn at least three major causes of the Civil War and how these causes impacted the later events in US history.
Metacognitive	Awareness of cognitive processes and how to use them	I will create a cause and effect graphic organizer to help me remember the information.
Affective	Feelings, emotions, enthusiasm, self-perception, self-concept, values, beliefs	Mr. Tanaka told me that I have the ability and brain power to learn anything. He said I just have to put my mind and energy into my studies and believe in myself.
Conative	Will, perseverance, persistence, determination, patience, tenacity, self-efficacy, intentionality	I am really having a difficult time with this assignment, but I am determined to write one of the best essays ever created on this topic.
Metaconative	The ethical application of "knowing" to learning and life, action directed toward the highest good, action intended to achieve a virtuous goal, ethical, moral behavior; honesty, respect, courage, integrity, responsibility, caring, empathy, trustworthiness	I did it because it was the ethical thing to do. Metaconation reminds us of the significance of our actions.

Figure 1.2

A Ticket to Ride

Your ticket to becoming a star teacher and learner is inside you, connected to your knowledge and beliefs. If you quietly look and listen you will see, hear, and feel the part of you that desires to shine, that wants you to be the best at what you do.

Who we are and what we choose to do with our learning and our lives resides in the power of the will. Covey (1990) explains, "The greatest gift we have is life and the next greatest gift is our ability to direct our lives."

applied to the learning process, but are distinctly different in terms of the philosophical and instructional focus.

Although we have described the domains in linear order, with separate and distinct attributes, we do not intend to rank the domains according to their importance in the learning process, nor do we wish to give the impression that the domains are independent of each other. To the contrary, the cognitive, affective, and conative domains are very much interconnected and interdependent.

Believing Is Seeing

When we see students as individuals charged with natural curiosity and filled with potential, we tend to provide them with opportunities to succeed, and we expect them to succeed. Consequently, students' will to succeed is engaged. This increases the likelihood that students learn the content and are imbued with the desire to continue to learn. On the other hand, if teachers communicate explicitly (with insensitive remarks) or implicitly (with closed body language or low expectations) that their students are hopeless or hapless, student success will be the exception rather than the rule. Our beliefs about who we are and who students are determine how we treat students and what and how we will or will not teach them. And these beliefs, unfortunately, will affect what students believe about themselves. Our beliefs are reflected in our actions. What we believe about students is what we see in them. A person's worldview is the paradigm through which they perceive reality.

Understanding that believing is seeing is essential to considering how success and failure are born and nurtured in the lives and minds of our students. *Success* begins with a belief. *Failure* begins with a belief. How students act upon specific beliefs informs us of how they see themselves, how they view school and the world around them. Our beliefs build our individual view of the world, creating our paradigm (see Figure 1.3).

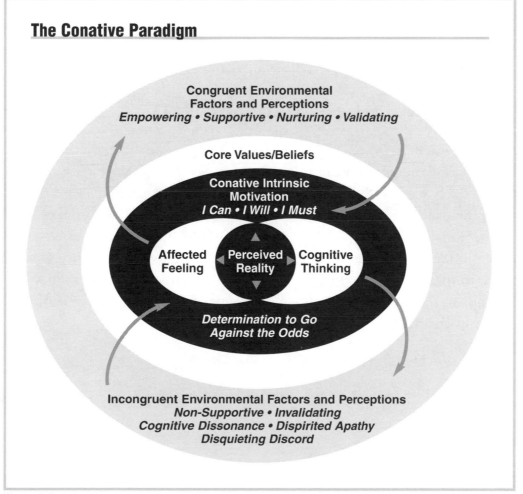

The Conative Paradigm

Congruent Environmental
Factors and Perceptions
Empowering • Supportive • Nurturing • Validating

Core Values/Beliefs

Conative Intrinsic
Motivation
I Can • I Will • I Must

Affected
Feeling

Perceived
Reality

Cognitive
Thinking

*Determination to Go
Against the Odds*

Incongruent Environmental Factors and Perceptions
*Non-Supportive • Invalidating
Cognitive Dissonance • Dispirited Apathy
Disquieting Discord*

Figure 1.3

Intentional Action

Intentional action—building upon the "winner within"—can be a powerful force in learning and can raise student performance in highly significant ways. According to Kolbe (1990), the "I will" factor is more important than IQ. Students have the power to accomplish amazing intellectual, social, ethical, and economic feats when they engage their conation. We all know stories from literature and real life of individuals who simply believed in themselves, worked toward specific goals, stayed focused, relentlessly persisted, challenged the status quo, and pushed themselves, and by so doing, created new ideas, methods, opportunities, technologies, medical breakthroughs, and social advances. The power of ordinary people to do extraordinary things for themselves and others is the nature of conation.

> In committed teacher-student learning communities, learners are engaged, not just put to work.

What Is Conative Intelligence (CI)?

Conative intelligence (CI) is the ability to persist, pursue, strive, and commit to a goal; understand the role of persistence in high performance; and productively engage the energy of the will in active teaching and learning. Effective learning communities seek to generate and sustain excellence. Conative intelligence embraces the will to succeed in all aspects of education and life. When people engage their conative intelligence, they strive to make wise, self-directed, cognitive, and affective choices. They also nurture, support, and energize their inner will to pursue personal and academic goals.

Core Components of Conative Intelligence

The nine components of conative intelligence demonstrate qualities inherent in successful students and teachers. Persons who display conative intelligence have a willingness to

- believe,
- understand,
- hope,
- strive,
- give,
- give up ineffective paradigms,
- focus,
- change, and
- pay exceptional attention to their own intentions.

Conative intelligence builds resilience. Resilient teachers and students demonstrate

- flexibility,
- optimism,
- endurance, and
- an openness to learn.

Resiliency is a personal trait of every successful leader and learner. Individuals who are resilient accept change more readily and recover more quickly from adverse situations, misfortune, and hardship. They live in the present but find comfort in looking toward the future. Conative intelligence increases our ability to capture and hold on to success through belief, energy, courage, conviction, and change (see Figure 1.4).

When the world around us seems fragile, dysfunctional, or impoverished, our belief, energy, courage, commitment, conviction, and change systems can become our gravity. They pull us down, hold us back, and reduce our personal expectations. Overcoming the dynamics of gravity requires the force of powerful engines that lift our systems of engagement and strengthen our capacity for learning. When all systems are "go," learning takes flight and we know where we are going.

✸

Using the Power of Conation

Belief	Stepping into the world of the will (conation)
Courage	Choosing to grow by finding personal meaning
Energy	Discovering your personal worth inside of you
Commitment	Changing as needed in order to learn, live, and become your personal best
Conviction	Inspiring others to learn and find themselves by your actions, choices, and expectations
Change	Transforming knowledge into wisdom

Figure 1.4

Lessons from

the **Heart**
of **Learning**

Throughout history, there are countless examples of individuals who, by their sheer will, tenacity, and determination, overcame barriers that seemed insurmountable, reached for goals that appeared to be unattainable, and confronted challenges that were much more terrifying than the proverbial "fire-eating dragon."

The following lessons, geared toward grades 9–12, acquaint students with two of these individuals. The lessons challenge students to reflect on the accomplishments of these individuals, so that the students might be motivated to establish and reach for their own goals and so that they might better understand the concept of conation.

(Note: To learn how to design lessons that reach the heart of learning, see chapter 4.)

If You Think You Can, You Can!

Without conation there is no product, only potential.

WHAT'S IT ALL ABOUT?

Purpose

* To become acquainted with the contributions to our society by individuals of various genders, cultures, and ethnicities
* To become aware of stereotypical attitudes
* To promote an understanding of one's ability to accomplish a desired goal in life
* To understand the power of the will

Instructional Objectives

* Students will develop independent research skills.
* Students will acquire and enhance comprehension, inference, and critical thinking skills.
* Students will gain knowledge of fiction and nonfiction historical events through biographies, narrative, and expository text.
* Students will utilize metacognitive skills.
* Students will gain an understanding of cognitive, affective, and conative skills.

Interdisciplinary Implementation

* History
* Language arts
* Library science
* Career education
* Technology

Instructional Focus

Students will read the biography of Elizabeth Blackwell and reflect on the following issues:

* Historical context or time period
* Society's attitudes about women, their roles, and their capabilities
* Women's attitudes and perceptions about their roles and capabilities

MAKING THE CONNECTION

Instructional Strategies and Activities

1. Place students in cooperative teams of three to five students.
2. Ask students to read the biography of Elizabeth Blackwell.
3. Challenge each team to complete a character trait web for Elizabeth. Explain that the web should list all of her attributes, skills, and talents.

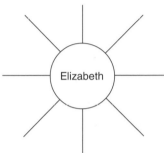

4. Encourage each team to share and compare their webs. Explain that each team should give a rationale for each trait they attributed to Dr. Blackwell.
5. Discuss the following questions with students:
   a. What do you think the statement "a socially prominent family" means?
   b. Why do you think Elizabeth did not want to conform to being a socially acceptable young lady?
   c. Would she be considered a nonconformist in today's society? Why or why not? Explain your response.
   d. What qualities or character traits do you think one would need to possess to be considered a "gracious lady" in the 1800s?
   e. Do you think the same qualities or character traits would apply now? Why or why not? Explain your response.
   f. Why do you think the Geneva Medical School accepted Elizabeth, while others rejected her application?
   g. Why do you think Elizabeth was persistent in her quest to become a doctor?
   h. Identify at least four qualities or character traits Elizabeth possessed that enabled her to never give up her dream of becoming a doctor.

Elizabeth Blackwell

Elizabeth Blackwell was born in 1821 into a socially prominent family. She was considered to be of "good breeding." Elizabeth did all of the social things expected of the young ladies in her position during this time period in history. However, she decided that she wanted her life to have more meaning than that of being a gracious lady who spent her days and evenings attending tea parties and other social events.

One of Elizabeth's friends, who understood Elizabeth's desire to do something useful with her life, suggested that Elizabeth go into the field of medicine. After much thought, Elizabeth decided to take a bold step and become a doctor. This was indeed a brave venture, because during this time, medicine was considered a man's domain. In fact, Elizabeth had to apply to several medical schools before she was finally accepted by the Geneva Medical School of New York. Needless to say, she had to face many hardships as she worked to complete her degree, but she persevered.

In 1849 she completed her training, graduated as the top student in her class, and became the first woman doctor in the United States. Her training served her country well, for when the Civil War began, she established a school to train nurses. These nurses treated and saved the lives of countless Union soldiers who were wounded in battle. She was the catalyst for other training programs that resulted in the availability of competent trained nurses for the Union army.

Elizabeth Blackwell died in 1910. She will always be remembered for her determination to become what she saw as her dream, in spite of what society had predestined for her. She practiced her right to be an individual and not only followed her dream, but turned that dream into a reality.

CONATIVE HOOK: Now that I *know,* what will I *do*?

Extended Research and Reflection

Encourage students to use the Internet to conduct research on the Geneva Medical School. Ask students to uncover the philosophy of the founders, the school's beliefs about the rights of women, the history of its admissions policy, the status of the school today, etc.

1. Encourage students to read, interpret, and discuss the following quote:

    Whenever there is a human being, I see God-given rights inherent in that being whatever may be the sex or complexion.—WILLIAM LLOYD GARRISON

2. Ask students to reflect on the question: What character traits, self-perceptions, or values do you have that will enable you to face and overcome challenges in school and life?

ASSESSMENT

Assess the success of the lesson by asking yourself the following questions:
1. Did students exhibit comprehension skills? How?
2. How well did students demonstrate their research skills?
3. Did students demonstrate the ability to work cooperatively in teams? How?
4. Were students able to apply literacy skills and critical thinking skills effectively? How was this evidenced?
5. Were students able to understand the underlying theme of being able to persevere in spite of the odds? How was this evidenced by each student?

If You Can Believe It, You Can Achieve It!

So many of our dreams at first seem impossible, then they seem improbable, and then, when we summon the will, they soon become inevitable.—CHRISTOPHER REEVE

WHAT'S IT ALL ABOUT?

Purpose
* To become acquainted with the contributions to our society by individuals of various genders, cultures, and ethnicities
* To become aware of stereotypical attitudes
* To promote an understanding of one's ability to accomplish a desired goal in life
* To understand the power of the will

Instructional Objectives
* Students will develop independent research skills.
* Students will acquire and enhance comprehension, inference, and critical thinking skills.
* Students will gain knowledge of fiction and nonfiction historical events through biographies, narrative, and expository text.
* Students will utilize metacognitive skills.
* Students will gain an understanding of cognitive, affective, and conative skills.

Interdisciplinary Implementation
* History
* Language arts
* Library science
* Career education
* Technology

Instructional Focus

Students will read the excerpt from the story "Jim Hill's Dream" and reflect on the following questions:

* Should a person have dreams or are dreams useless?
* How does a dream help a person achieve his or her goal?
* Do you believe dreams can come true?

Jim Hill's Dream
by James Bruchac

Jim Hill and Larry Jackson stood waiting for the subway to take them to the park.

"Man, I can't take this heat today," Jim said, wiping the sweat off his forehead.

"I don't know what's worse, the heat or the smell of this place. I hate the subway in August," Larry said. A moment later, the subway arrived, and Jim and Larry grabbed two seats. Ten minutes later, they were walking the two blocks to the park.

"So, Jim, you still got that crazy idea of playing football?" Larry asked as they walked. "Practice starts tomorrow, doesn't it?"

Jim hesitated. "Sure I'm going to do it," he said. "It's either now or never." Jim tried to hide his nervousness. He had trained all summer for his first season of football, and practice started tomorrow.

"You'd better get used to the heat, Jimmy boy. I hear Coach Long works his team till they drop, without even a water break," Larry said.

"It couldn't get any hotter than my grandfather's sweat lodge," Jim said with a smile.

"What's a sweat lodge?" Larry asked.

Jim explained a Native American sweat lodge as simply as he could. He told Larry that it was like a church because you prayed a lot—for yourself, other people in the lodge, the earth, future generations, or anything else you felt the need to pray for. He explained how the red-hot rocks in the middle of the lodge brought you closer to the earth and helped burn away impurities.

"How do you feel afterward?" Larry asked.

"Like a newborn baby," Jim answered.

He thought back to the time he had seen his grandfather two summers ago. Every other year, Jim and his family visited his grandparents in the country. His grandfather was with him the first time he was in a sweat lodge. He told Jim the stories of his Native American ancestors. They were often amusing, but they also taught lessons and told of bravery, overcoming great odds, and finding the strength within your heart to meet any challenge.

The stories encouraged Jim to finally try out for the football team. His friends said he was too small to play football, but he had gained fifteen pounds over the last year and had grown to over six feet. They still tried to discourage him, though, saying it was too late to try out for a new sport in his junior year.

"All the good players started in grade school. If you even make the team, you'll just sit on the bench," one friend had said.

Jim tried hard to ignore the comments, but they were always in the back of his mind. He knew it would be hard to start playing football at his age, but he was determined to try.

As Tamara and Amanda, the boys' girlfriends, approached, Larry said, "Well, today is Jim's last day before he starts football—his last day of summer and freedom." He gave Jim a light punch in the arm.

"I think it's great that Jim's trying out for the team," said Amanda.

"As long as he stays in one piece," said Tamara.

Jim smiled and took Tamara's hand as they walked toward the pond at the center of the park. Jim knew it was his last day of relaxation for a while, and he cherished every moment of it.

Early the next morning, Jim headed over to the football locker room for the first pre-season meeting. As he approached the gym, he began to doubt his decision.

"This is crazy," he said to himself. He paused for a moment, realizing that all he had to do was turn around and go home. But he thought of a story he had been told as a child, the story of the seventh direction. In the story, after the places of the six directions in the world were given—north, south, east, west, sky, and earth—the animals had to decide where to hide the most powerful of all directions, the seventh direction. This direction was the most powerful because anyone who discovered it could never truly be defeated.

After many animals had made suggestions, it was decided that the best place to hide the seventh direction was within the human heart because it was the last place most people would look. When found, its power would be unstoppable. As Jim remembered this lesson, he thought of that strength within his own heart and how important it was for him to try out for the team.

"This is it. My last chance at a dream. I can't give up now," he thought as he continued toward the building.

MAKING THE CONNECTION

Instructional Strategies and Activities

1. Place students in cooperative teams of three to five students.
2. Ask students to read "Jim Hill's Dream."
3. Challenge each team to complete the following attribute webs, using information, clues, and inferences provided by the author of the story. Explain that the team must provide the verb in the last web.

    Jim *acts* like . . . .

    _____

    Jim *feels* like . . . .

    _____

    Jim *thinks* like . . . .

    _____

    Jim _____ like . . . .

    _____

4. Encourage each team to share and discuss their webs.
5. Ask teams to discuss and answer the following questions:
    a. What is the setting of this story? How do you know?
    b. What do you think Jim's cultural background is? What was the clue(s) that led you to your conclusion?
    c. What kind of feelings do you think Jim had about his grandfather? Give a rationale for your answer.
    d. What were three qualities Jim's grandfather taught him?
    e. How do you think this story ended?
6. Tell teams to share and compare their answers.

CONATIVE HOOK: Now that I *know*, what will I *do*?

Extended Research and Reflection

1. Tell students to re-read the Christopher Reeve quote from the beginning of the lesson. Challenge students to explain what the quote means, using personal examples or experiences.

2. Ask students to interview someone they know—a friend, a family member, a neighbor, or even a teacher—about the hopes or aspirations they had or currently have. Tell students to develop a series of three to five interview questions that will require the interviewee to think about, explore, and share their stories.

3. Encourage students to write about their own dreams and aspirations. Challenge them to reflect on how they plan to make their dreams come true.

ASSESSMENT

Assess the success of the lesson by asking yourself the following questions:

- Did students exhibit comprehension skills? Explain how.
- Were students able to understand the importance of having future aspirations and ways to fulfill them? How was this demonstrated?
- Did students demonstrate their writing skills? How was this skill exhibited?
- How did students demonstrate that they understood what is meant by "Where there's a will, there's a way"?

FURTHER READING

Cooke, G. (2002). *Keys to success for urban school principals.* Arlington Heights, IL: SkyLight Professional Development.

Edmonds, R. (1979). Effective schools for the urban poor. *Educational Leadership, 37,* 15–24.

Goleman, D. (1995). *Emotional intelligence: Why it can matter more than IQ for character, health and lifelong achievement.* New York: Bantam.

Kessler, R. (2000). *The soul of education: Helping students find connection, compassion, and character at school.* Alexandria, VA: Association for Supervision and Curriculum Development.

Kohl, H. (1991). *I won't learn from you!: The role of assent in learning.* Minneapolis: Milkweed.

Miller, J. P. (2002). *Education and the soul: Toward a spiritual curriculum.* Albany: State University of New York.

Senge, P. M. (1990). *The fifth discipline: The art and practice of the learning organization.* New York: Doubleday.

Where Learning Lives

Student

When I think about one of the best lessons I learned in school so far, it is the lesson that **"being me"** is okay. Just being me was always hard, because everyone used to doubt me and tell me I would never be anything in life. Finding myself took a lot of work and **courage.** It took time to find out what I was good at and what I needed help with.

In the 7th grade, my teacher told me, "Don't ever let anyone doubt you because you are an intelligent young lady." Since then, I took that to heart, forgetting about everyone that doubted me, telling myself that **I could be anything** I want to be in life. That's why being me is the best thing I learned.—ELEMENTARY STUDENT

Teacher

Creating an environment that encourages risk taking and positive attitudes toward one another, as well as with oneself, begins when the students enter the classroom on the first day of school. As my students create a classroom "bill of rights," they realize they are being **empowered with the ability to control their own destiny.** They will be making choices that will affect them as learners, friends, and most importantly as individuals. This enhances their inner will to **think positively about themselves.** To reinforce this thought we have our classroom motto, "If I Think I Can, I Can!," which is said after the pledge and is displayed in the room as a banner.

The students know I will not give up on them and they cannot give up on themselves! I know we have succeeded when students encourage one another in the classroom by saying, **"You can do it!"** or "If you think you can do it, you will." This wonderful encouragement demonstrates an intrinsic understanding of believing in oneself and processing the will to try.—HIGH SCHOOL TEACHER

What Is Learning?

Authentic learning is a conscious exercise, starting with who we are and evolving into all that we become. In order for students to succeed in academics (or in life), they first need help in discovering the ability to learn within themselves. Second, they must acquire or build their courage to learn.

"The Thinking Curriculum" (NCREL) defines learning as "the active, goal-directed construction of meaning. This definition of learning takes a constructive, perceptive, metacognitive, connective, and transformative view." The Greek definition for education is leading another out of darkness or ignorance. To set the learning process in motion, the teacher must have the desire to lead. The foundation of teaching is the simple, yet powerful, belief that one can teach and others can learn. Teachers have the ability to foster students' learning and build their courage to learn through everyday lessons in regular classrooms. We call this authentic teaching and learning.

Learning in the Conative Domain

Over the past two decades, we've discovered much about the way the brain learns. For example, we know that the brain makes meaning by

Leading the Way

Teachers and mentors are on the cutting edge of students' lives. Teachers are the ones who will lead the way, who open students' hearts as well as their minds. When our young rise, the world will note that their success was cultivated by how we chose to be their examples—what we chose to be to them and for them.

finding connections and that emotions play a large role in memory and recall (Wolfe, 2001). In addition to what we've learned about brain physiology, we've also learned about how the brain works through the study of conation. For example, we know that before learning takes place two things must happen: the learner must choose to learn and the learner must have enough courage to make the choice to learn. Making the choice to learn is influenced by the learner's perception of herself, her perception of the world around her, her beliefs, how she interprets what she knows or thinks she knows, and how she chooses to respond to what she believes. Perseverance is the single most important conative component. Figure 2.1 offers a number of reflection questions that can be used at different stages of learning. You and your students may use the questions to reflect upon how you perceive the role of perseverance in your lives. This type of reflection is called *metaconation*.

> Courageous learning involves moments of intensity that take students beyond ordinary outcomes.

Choice in a Conative Context

Sometimes the conative difference between choosing for or against learning, living, and succeeding lies simply in giving oneself permission to learn, grow, and become. Our challenge is to help students make the conative connection by using realistic, yet challenging, goals and strategies that foster students' desire to learn.

The greater the correlation between one's personal want or need to know and one's willingness to learn a particular concept or subject, the stronger the possibility that the task will be attempted and possibly learned. Kohl (1991) maintains that some students make a conscious decision not to learn and that these students present an intellectual and social challenge. These would-be learners—those who are not yet interested nor committed to studying—are kept out of the learning game by default. Unfortunately, they are often also left out of the rigors of the game of life as well.

The Perseverance Factor

- Am I willing to persevere to learn?
- Am I persevering?
- Why am I persevering?
- How have I changed as a result of my perseverance?
- Next steps?
  Beneath a question is not always an answer but perhaps another question—more powerful than the one preceding it. Pushing for answers in a classroom is not always the issue. Students often learn on much deeper levels when given time to ponder thoughtful considerations that seek depth and richness.

Figure 2.1

Personal belief and willingness are elemental and relational factors that tend to promote or inhibit one's desire to strive. These two factors, belief and willingness, are affective and conative variables that play a significant role in learning. One's choice to enter the learning process and then involve oneself in the pursuit of learning involves personal and academic choices. A belief in one's ability to learn and a willingness to participate in the act of learning as a means to achieve a specific goal are the first steps on the journey that leads to authentic success.

Teachers should help students become aware that they must make an affirmative choice to learn. Teachers can use Figure 2.2: Your Conative Profile to help students recognize the connection between will and success. The lesson at the end of this chapter entitled "If I Had a Choice, I Would Be . . . " can also help students harness the power of conation.

After making the choice to learn, the learner must amass the courage to act on the choice. The next section discusses the role of courage in the learning process.

What Is Courage?

Courage is *wisdom* connected to *will*. This connection sparks action. Whether or not an individual decides to act is dependent upon that individual's

- belief,
- knowledge,
- wisdom, and
- will.

Belief. Simply put, belief is accepting as true something for which there may or may not be subjective proof. The beliefs we hold, whether deliberately chosen or instilled, create a model for interpreting and structuring our perception of what is real and what we can do as a result.

Knowledge. Today, the meaning of the word *knowledge* is debatable. For the sake of this discussion, knowledge is a collection of information. Each piece of information is a facet through which the world is perceived by a particular individual.

Wisdom. We can think of wisdom as being synonymous with sound judgment. Wisdom provides responsible direction to the will. In other words, wisdom, when infused with will, leads to responsible action. If will

THE **Will** to **Teach**

Taking a Heroic Journey

Educating a life! What an awesome thought—to touch hearts and minds in amazing ways, build lives, and mold futures. By the time our students reach eighteen, they will hear and encounter tens of thousands of voices, philosophies, and controversial issues. Some thoughts will be rejected, others embraced, and some will be remembered only as unobtrusive rumblings of everyday life.

Your Conative Profile

What is your conative profile? Who's in charge of your life? How strong is your will? To aid in determining the degree in which your engage your *will* in goal attainment, this instrument will assist you in identifying areas of conative strengths and conative needs.

There are two sections to the profile. Read each item in each section and circle the number that best represents your answer. Upon completion of each section, add the numbers that represent your responses. Place your subtotal at the end of each section. Upon completion of the profile, add subtotals of both sections to get your total score.

Section 1

Please rate statements 1–13 as follows: 5=strongly agree; 4=agree; 3=undecided; 2=disagree; and 1=strongly disagree.

1. You remain focused on your goals at all times........................5 4 3 2 1

2. You believe in yourself..5 4 3 2 1

3. You believe that you can achieve anything you set out to do.............5 4 3 2 1

4. You are a risk taker...5 4 3 2 1

5. You feel that there is room for improvement within yourself.............5 4 3 2 1

6. You believe that when necessary, going against the odds is important.....5 4 3 2 1

7. You attempt to do your best at all times.............................5 4 3 2 1

8. You continue to work toward your goal after being told that the
   task is impossible..5 4 3 2 1

9. You put on a take-charge spirit ("I can, I will, I must") and then act
   upon your beliefs..5 4 3 2 1

10. When you know you have made the right decision, you act upon your
    beliefs, even when others' beliefs are distinctly different from yours.......5 4 3 2 1

11. You find yourself accomplishing tasks that others might not try..........5 4 3 2 1

12. You find yourself turning stumbling blocks into stepping stones..........5 4 3 2 1

13. You tend to focus on what you want in life and go after it with all of
    your mental and physical energy. 5 4 3 2 1

Section 1 Subtotal.._____

Figure 2.2

Section 2

Please rate statements 14–20 as follows: 1=strongly agree; 2=agree; 3=undecided; 4=disagree; 5=strongly disagree. ***Be careful! The rating system is opposite from the rating system used for the statements in Section 1.***

14. You feel that you become a weaker person when you are criticized for your beliefs. 1 2 3 4 5

15. You believe that there is simply nothing that you can do to improve your present situation. 1 2 3 4 5

16. You generally want others to take on leadership responsibilities, because you feel they probably know more than you do. 1 2 3 4 5

17. You feel that your ideas are not important; therefore, you dismiss them. . . . 1 2 3 4 5

18. You find that you spend most of your time just trying to "get by." 1 2 3 4 5

19. You try to maintain the status quo (i.e., "Good enough is good enough"). . . 1 2 3 4 5

20. You find yourself immobilized when others don't agree with your opinions. 1 2 3 4 5

Section 2 Subtotal . . . . _____

TOTAL FOR SECTION 1 + SECTION 2 SCORE: . . . . _____

Scoring

Remember, as you strengthen your locus of control, personal beliefs, knowledge, skills and determination, you develop personal tools you can use to change the direction of your learning and your life. Learning and life are personal experiences, requiring personal engagement and lifelong initiatives and committments.

89–100 Great! You're in the driver's seat. Enjoy the journey while empowering others to join you along the way.

76–88 Awaken your take-charge spirit. Take charge of your learning and your life. Create new experiences for yourself that will allow you to explore life to its fullest. Stretch and grow from your triumphs and your challenges.

0–75 You need a lift. Lifts are good; we all need them. They give us a better view of ourselves and the world. Discover ways to find a more positive sense of self and perspective of life. What do you want to do with your life? What are your goals? Take charge and make changes where needed. Shift your paradigm and experience more joy, success, and personal fulfillment in life and in learning. Become the experience you've been looking for. Express your ability to be remarkable. Choose more than near life experiences. Do something amazing. This is your time. This is your turn. This is your life—Lift it up— Go for it!

proceeds without wisdom, negative outcomes may be the result. Wisdom sets the direction and it positions learning at the center of action. Acting with wisdom (good judgment) lifts us up by strengthening our determination and by helping us interpret our life experiences. Acting with a lack of wisdom holds us back.

Will (conation). When we look at the role of the will in terms of courage (or lack of courage), we discover that our courage is affected by what we believe about ourselves and how we interpret life experiences and the world around us. Being courageous depends on what we choose to believe. For our purposes, the will moves knowledge from thought to action.

Why focus on the will? The will is the center of action and behavior. Through our will, the world discovers who we truly are and how we've combined our beliefs, knowledge, and (hopefully) wisdom and directed

The Seeds of Learning

Take a moment to think about a tiny seed and reflect upon how it grows. At first sight, the seed looks hard, and possibly worthless. If you didn't know it was a seed, you might never suspect that within its walls resided the substance of life.

Just as seeds need nourishment to break through their shells and sprout—so do our students need nourishment to grow. Each student is similar to a seed, waiting to be nourished. When we think of students as seeds, we realize that they are complete within themselves, that they have within them the power to grow and mature. However, just like seeds, students need the proper environment and nourishment to grow and thrive.

them toward productive goals. We will examine the impact of these four factors and others when looking more closely at what moves individuals toward or away from a specific goal in chapter 3.

Gholar and Riggs' Conative Taxonomy

For decades, researchers have relied on Bloom's taxonomy (Bloom et al., 1956), an instructional tool designed to allow teachers to determine the six levels of higher-order thinking skills. In comparison, we have created a conative taxonomy, an evaluative tool designed to enable teachers to assess levels of

The will is the search engine that seeks and creates meaning, making connections to what I will choose to learn and do with what I am learning.

student engagement in the learning process. The fundamental framework for the conative taxonomy of self-directed learning includes these elements: *personal discovery, transition, transformation,* and *transcendency.* These elements are described in Figure 2.3.

Students engage or disengage their will to learn based on their perception of reality. Students want to know: "What's in it for me?" If they feel or believe that learning is worth their effort, they will put forth the effort and more, sometimes exceeding established goals.

Authentic Success

Authentic teaching and learning produces an educational environment wherein students are seldom solely motivated to perform with the promise of material rewards. The challenge of achieving a task becomes its own reward. Authentic learning occurs in the conative domain. Learning is perceived as relevant, important, and full of meaning. Students stretch, grow, and move beyond their prior limits. The development of their perceptual capacity tends to increase. They see themselves as capable and make observable movement toward mutually shared goals. Figure 2.4 shows the characteristics of authentic learning that help students succeed in school and in life.

Gholar and Riggs' Conative Taxonomy

Transcendency

At this level students and teachers possess the will to

- give voice to ideas and issues that matter most,
- rise above old paradigms that are no longer useful,
- take an ethical stand in uncomfortable situations,
- encourage others to strive, believe, and release the past (if necessary) in order to renew their relationships with learning and life, and
- be a light in dark places.

Transformation

At this level students and teachers possess the will to

- live fully and become their personal best,
- increase positive learning experiences,
- experience learning as its own personal reward, and
- transform knowledge into wisdom.

Transition

At this level students and teachers possess the will to

- engage fully in learning,
- change,
- focus and remain focused on an expected goal,
- produce quality work (students) and quality teaching experiences (teachers), and
- open themselves to authentic learning and teaching.

Personal discovery

At this level students and teachers possess the will to

- value themselves as learners (students) or leaders (teachers),
- value learning,
- see beyond today,
- succeed, and
- appreciate themselves through their own eyes.

Figure 2.3

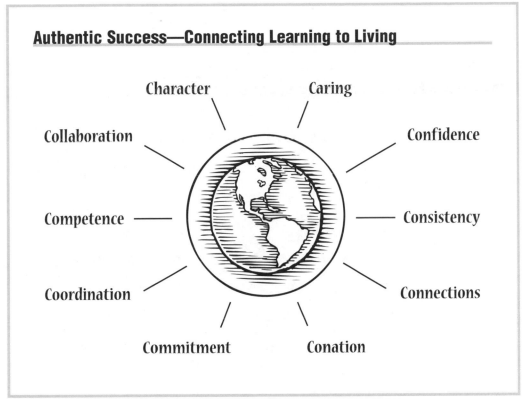

Authentic Success—Connecting Learning to Living

Character
Caring
Collaboration
Confidence
Competence
Consistency
Coordination
Connections
Commitment
Conation

Figure 2.4

Character Education and the Conative Spirit of Learning

During childhood, students acquire the bricks and mortar to fashion the foundation for character building. This foundation will serve them throughout their lives. If the edifice is solid, students will thrive. They will learn, grow, and become responsible individuals who demonstrate courage, respect, and integrity.

Parents are a child's first and most significant character educators. Whether modeling the Golden Rule, emphasizing the importance of honesty, demonstrating the power of perseverance by staying with a task until it is done, or showing concern for those less fortunate, most parents try their best to teach their sons and daughters the essential lessons of character.

Go Team!

Some believe the distance between the learners and the expectations that have been established for their learning are simply too far apart, unattainable, and unrealistic. As educators, our conative role is to teach students how to shorten this distance. We can do so by being external cheerleaders and by encouraging students to become their own internal cheerleaders. Through literature, videos, movies, and other experiences, we can teach students how they can fight and win battles, especially battles to overcome the odds in school, and most importantly, in life.

What Is Character?

A popular definition of character is "what we do when no one else is around." We often think that a person's character is "tested" in response to various challenges, temptations, or ethical dilemmas. (For example, we determine we won't cheat even when no one else is around.) Other definitions refer to character as a moral compass or one's capacity to draw the line where none exists.

Character, from the Greek word *charakter,* has come to mean the constellation of strengths and weaknesses that form and reveal who we are. Our character does not consist of a single statement or a random act of generosity, but it comprises our everyday qualities and dispositions—both good and bad. Assessing our character involves taking an inventory of what we spend most of our time thinking about and doing.

Character Education

Sometimes called social and emotional learning (ASCD, 1997), character education provides lessons in character building. These practices have the potential to transform ethical ambiguity into ethical clarity and moral action. Service learning, mentoring, peer mediation, and student leadership are among the programs that successfully increase students' social and emotional intelligence (Barr & Parrett, 2003; ASCD, 1997). Education emphasizes the responsibilities and benefits of productive living in a global and diverse society. Character education prepares students to come face-to-face with the realities of life and equips them with the tools they need to make ethically sound decisions and responsible choices in a world of challenge, opportunity, and change.

THE **Will** to **Teach**

Making Heartfelt Connections

In the conative domain, we engage students in realizing their dreams by bolstering their courage and their will to learn. We help students strive for success by giving light and sharing personal meaning as they move forward on the path to knowledge.

Academic success is embodied in the will to learn—to know, strive, believe, interact, initiate, risk, respond, and fully engage in the process of learning. Courageous teaching involves the same connections. We need connections that matter, connections that are heartfelt. We need to connect (or reconnect) to our ideals. We can connect by engaging in human moments, moments that occur when two individuals pay attention to one another.

Courage, Character, and Conation

The stamp of conscience is the will. Our identity resides in what we value—what we believe is just, true, fair, responsible, and good for all individuals. Our identity is imprinted by our courage, character, and conation. Courage, character, and conation help us to make a difference and make our presence felt through positive contributions to our world. These qualities bring us together. They make us one.

Do we need courage? Do we need character? Do we need conation? Each generation answers these questions in their own way. We teach our students the importance of these values by the way we live, by our daily interactions with them, by the verbal and nonverbal messages they receive from us.

A majority of Americans share a respect for the fundamental traits of character—honesty, compassion, justice, courage, generosity, perseverance, self-discipline, responsibility, respect, and caring. Yet, in contemporary culture, many of our youth feel uncertain when faced with issues of right and wrong. Young people have even more difficulty when faced with choices at a higher level of decision making—when they must choose between right and right. Ambiguous actions on the part of youth and an inability to understand or care about relationships or the human condition are in themselves ethical dilemmas. Harvard scholar and psychologist Robert Coles (1997) postulates that children possess an innate desire to learn the difference between right and wrong and to observe models of moral behavior. Students look to the adults in their lives for wisdom, hope, and meaning.

Through character education, students gain insight into what is important and what is not. As they make choices and seek to fulfill their dreams, students learn to respect themselves, others, and the world around them. When taught to live their lives in an ethical manner they develop resilience and a sense of purpose. Lessons taught at home stay with students as they make their way through school and life.

Conation, courage, and character—in one voice, together we speak!

❋

We need to examine more closely the power of the will. It might change how we think about learning, and what we will practice.

THE **Will** to **Teach**

Flight Training

In conative classrooms, teaching and learning are like flight training—students learn to take off with new ideas. Teachers who are inspired to continue their own journeys lift students' minds and hearts and motivate them to achieve to their highest potential. As students become more self-confident and willing to be persistent in their academic studies, they climb to higher and higher take off points. As they become more and more willing to learn and grow, they take off and fly.

Lessons from

the **Heart** of **Learning**

Students are sometimes overlooked as individuals who have strong feelings and emotions, as well as hopes and dreams. Many of them conceal their hurt and pain because they feel adults will not understand or simply do not care. They often hesitate to take the risk of sharing their aspirations for fear of being ridiculed.

The following lessons encourage students to explore and express their emotions through positive and creative channels. Through these activities, they are urged to reflect on their challenges and/or think about the future, while keeping in mind that they have the talents, skills, and will to overcome adversaries.

(Note: To learn how to design lessons that reach the heart of learning, see chapter 4.)

It's Not Always What It Seems to Be!

You see it's like a portmanteau—there are two meanings packed into one word. —Lewis Carroll

WHAT'S IT ALL ABOUT?

Purpose

* To enhance understanding of metaphors
* To promote creative writing through the use of metaphors
* To use personal experiences and knowledge as a foundation for creating poems and compositions

Instructional Objectives

* Students will learn how to use metaphors.
* Students will strengthen their writing and higher-order thinking skills.
* Students will acquire new vocabulary words.

Interdisciplinary Implementation

* Language arts
* Social studies
* Science

Instructional Focus

Students will learn about metaphors and will read the poem "Song of a Dandelion" and reflect upon the following questions:

* Do you think the student poet was writing about dandelions? Why or why not?
* What message is the author trying to convey through metaphor?
* Is it easier to express emotions using metaphors?

MAKING THE CONNECTION

Instructional Strategies and Activities

1. Discuss and define the word *metaphor.* Explain that authors use metaphors to make stories and poetry more interesting and fun to read.

2. Place students in teams of three to five students. To ensure that students understand the concept of a metaphor, challenge them to think of a few examples of metaphors with their teams. Stress that the metaphors can be about anything in their lives or personal experiences or can even center around their subjects in school, such as language arts, science, and math. Following are some sample metaphors:
   - Algebra is a bone-crushing headache.
   - The color blue is a cool, refreshing wave on the hottest day of the year.
   - The human brain is a computer with an infinite amount of memory.
   - The character's mouth was a garbage can.

3. Encourage teams to share their metaphors. As teams share, ask the class to interpret the meaning of each metaphor.

4. Continue the dialogue about the usage of metaphors, providing additional examples if needed.

5. Encourage students to silently re-read the poem "Song of a Dandelion Pushing up Through an Urban Sidewalk Crack."

6. Ask students:
   a. Do you think the author was writing only about dandelions?
   b. Could this poem be a metaphor about something or someone else?

Call students' attention to specific lines or words in the poem (e.g., "No other flowers can mimic our style" or "atmosphere" or other significant words or phrases). Students will likely be able to conclude that this poem could be about homeless or economically disadvantaged people or students who are not smart, attractive, or popular.

Song of a Dandelion Pushing up
Through an Urban Sidewalk Crack

We sprout up boldly through the cracks to offer beauty that the sidewalk lacks.

And spread our sunshine-bright yellow smiles.

No other flowers can mimic our style.

They call us weeds, but we are a gift sent from heaven to brighten
and uplift the sad, gray atmosphere.

No other flowers dare to grow around here.

If you would stop and simply see our beauty compared to the misery
. . . the dirt and pieces of broken glass and useless things that litter
the grass,

You would not see us as simply weeds, but as beings that a
city needs.

Yes, we smile defiantly anyway, and flash our smile to
boldly display what joy can come from the little things.

We are a song, and if you listen, we sing.

—HIGH SCHOOL STUDENT

CONATIVE HOOK: Now that I *know*, what will I *do*?

Extended Research and Reflection

Challenge each team to create a metaphor that focuses on a social issue or some topic of interest to them. Tell teams to create a story or poem based on the metaphor they created. Encourage teams to share their poems or stories with the class.

Ask Students

- To share positive ways to express frustration
- What characters in movies, novels, or plays that they are familiar with have shown perseverance

ASSESSMENT

Assess the success of the lesson by asking yourself the following questions:

1. Did students demonstrate their understanding of metaphors? How?
2. Were students able to work cooperatively in teams to develop their poems or stories? How was this cooperation demonstrated?
3. Did students exhibit creativity and critical thinking skills? How?
4. Were students able to demonstrate their knowledge of strategies for dealing with difficult situations?

If I Had a Choice, I Would Be ...

A failure establishes only this, that our determination to succeed was not strong enough—JOHN CHRISTIAN BOVEE

WHAT'S IT ALL ABOUT?

Purpose
* To enhance students' awareness of their creative abilities
* To tap into students' multiple intelligences
* To probe students' prior knowledge of science concepts

Instructional Objectives
* Students will use their prior knowledge.
* Students will implement math and science concepts.
* Students will enhance their literacy skills.
* Students will develop their comprehension skills.

Interdisciplinary Implementation
* Science
* Language arts
* Vocabulary
* Technology

Instructional Focus
Students will read *The Very Hungry Caterpillar* by Eric Carle and reflect upon the following issues:
* If you had the choice to do or be anything, what would you do or be?
* Why would you choose to do that?
* Can you attain this if you put all your effort into it?

MAKING THE CONNECTION

Instructional Strategies and Activities

1. Begin by reading the book *The Very Hungry Caterpillar* or a similar story. Read the title of the book, show students the cover, and ask inferential and comprehension questions such as:
   - What do you think this story is going to be about?
   - Is a caterpillar an animal or an insect?
   - Can you name some other kinds of insects?
   - Who can describe what a caterpillar looks like?
   - Has anyone ever held a caterpillar? How does it feel?

2. Read the story aloud. When you are finished reading, ask students these questions:
   - Do you think the caterpillar was happy being a caterpillar? Why or why not?
   - What do you think the caterpillar might want to be if he could be something different? Explain why.
   - Are you happy being who you are? Why or why not?

3. Divide the class into four cooperative teams. Encourage each team to select two choices from If I Had a Choice (on the following page). Ask teams to draw pictures of their selections.

4. When students have completed their drawings, challenge each team to do the following:
   - Tell why you chose your two insects.
   - Describe the insects you chose.
   - Explain all you know about your insects.
   - Display your drawings.

Extended Research and Reflection

Challenge teams to select one of their insects and complete a Venn diagram, comparing and contrasting the differences and similarities between their insect and another team's insect. Provide appropriate grade-level science books or Internet resources available to aid the students. On page 57 is an example Venn diagram:

If I Had a Choice, I Would Be . . .

If I had a choice, I would be an *ant*, because

_____.

_____.

If I had a choice, I would be a *butterfly,* because

_____.

_____.

If I had a choice, I would be a *honey bee,* because

_____.

_____.

If I had a choice, I would be a *caterpillar,* because

_____.

_____.

If I had a choice, I would be a *mosquito,* because

_____.

_____.

If I had a choice, I would be an *earthworm,* because

_____.

_____.

If I had a choice, I would be a *spider,* because

_____.

_____.

If I had a choice, I would be a *fly,* because

_____.

_____.

Comparing and Contrasting Earthworms and Honey Bees

EARTHWORMS

HONEY BEES

(How Earthworms Are Different from Honey Bees)

(How Earthworms and Honey Bees Are the Same)

(How Honey Bees Are Different from Earthworms)

1. Earthworms live in the ground.
2. Earthworms get around by crawling.
3. Earthworms are used for fishing bait.

1. Both are insects.
2. Both are useful to humans.

1. Honey bees live above the ground.
2. Honey bees get around by flying.
3. Honey bees make honey that we can eat.

Ask students the following questions so that they may reflect upon what they learned in this lesson:

* Did this lesson help you learn more about insects? How?
* Did this lesson help you learn more about yourself? How?

ASSESSMENT

Assess the success of the lesson by asking yourself the following questions:

- Did students gain an understanding of and enhance their knowledge about insects? How was this knowledge attainment determined?
- Were students able to use their prior knowledge and various cognitive and creative skills with this activity? How?
- Were students able to demonstrate their comprehension skills? How?

FURTHER READING

Allee, V. (1997). *The knowledge evolution.* Newton, MA: Butterworth-Heinemann.

Coles, R. (1997). *The moral intelligence of children.* New York: Random.

Damon, W. (Ed.). (2002). *Bringing in a new era in character education.* Stanford, CA: Hoover Institution.

Jensen, E. (1998). *Teaching with the brain in mind.* Alexandria, VA: Association for Supervision and Curriculum Development.

Kolb, D. A. (1984). *Experiential learning: Experience as the source of learning and development.* Englewood Cliffs, NJ: Prentice-Hall.

Senge, P. M., et al. (1994). *The fifth discipline fieldbook: Strategies and tools for building a learning organization.* New York: Currency, Doubleday.

Skinner, B. F. (1989). The origins of cognitive thought. *American Psychologist, 44,* 13–18.

Smith, C. P. (Ed.). (1992). *Motivation and personality: Handbook of thematic content analysis.* New York: Cambridge University Press.

Woods, D. R. (1994). *Problem-based learning: How to gain the most from PBL.* Waterdown, Ontario, Canada: Donald R. Woods.

Woodward, W. R. (1982). The "discovery" of social behaviorism and social learning theory, 1870–1980. *American Psychologist, 37,* 396–410.

An Invitation to Learn

Student

My teacher believes in me. She says encouraging things to me every day. I have the kind of teacher who makes all of the students in our class want to learn. She's really quite funny, but she also gets down to business. I'm always learning something new. It's great that she knows how to make learning fun. I scored well on my Iowa Test.

—THIRD GRADE STUDENT

Teacher

Caring is one of the most indefinable personal qualities, but it is one of the most important for a teacher.

—HIGH SCHOOL TEACHER

The Hidden Curriculum

Students are acutely aware of what Dewey (1933) called the "hidden curriculum" that stems from classroom interactions between teachers and students and between students and other students. When these interactions are characterized by safety, cooperation, and respect, the learning environment tends to be inviting, welcoming, and stimulating. The environment also promotes conation and self-recognition.

Inviting Success

Inviting success begins with a clear understanding of issues, challenges, questions, and choices that students face daily at school and in the community. Many educators (and others) often discuss what students need to know and be able to do in order to lead successful lives. However, we

Faith in Human Potential

What are we teachers willing to do to ensure that we have given our all to bring out the best in students? We must be clear about our guiding principles. We must ask ourselves, "What beliefs guide my actions?" Real teaching comes from a deep faith in the human capacity to grow and learn. It emanates from a strong belief in one's purpose and a willingness to express one's convictions in various ways throughout the scope of one's work. Learning involves more than placing a task on the table and saying, "This is what we are going to learn today," and assume that it will be learned.

educators must take time to focus on ourselves: what we believe about our roles and our goals as educators. Purkey and Novak (1984) in *Inviting School Success* suggest extending invitations to students in order to make students feel welcome to the educational community. They outline four levels of invitation that impact directly on the academic growth and accomplishments of students. Figure 3.1 outlines the four levels. The levels are also described in the following paragraphs.

Purkey's Levels of Inviting

Intentionally Inviting
- effort
- awareness

Unintentionally Inviting
- professionalism
- respect

Unintentionally Disinviting
- insensitivity
- low challenge

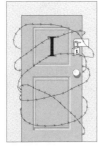

Intentionally Disinviting
- hostility
- demeaning
- accusatory language

From *Inviting School Success* by Purkey & Novak (1978). Adapted with permission of Wadsworth, an imprint of the Wadsworth Group, a division of Thomson Learning. Fax: 800-730-2215.

Figure 3.1

"Disinviting" Versus Inviting

Levels 1 and 2—intentionally and unintentionally *"disinviting"*—require students to devise, create, develop, and/or enhance their own skills, talents, self-beliefs, and sheer will to overcome the proverbial beast of defeatism. They must rely on their inner strength to self-motivate. In other words, they must call upon their conative spirit and firmly believe in their own abilities to cope, survive, and succeed emotionally, psychologically, and academically. When the school environment does not invite and welcome students with accommodating, compassionate, and supportive behaviors, actions, and instructional activities, then students must "crash the party" without the benefit of a formal invitation and, with resolve and determination, make themselves welcomed and part of the event. Students must summon conation in its basic form—they must fuel their internal engines so that they can summon the courage, resilience, will, and staying power to "hang in there."

> A brave person is not one who is never afraid, but one who takes a stand, prepared and willing to advance or retreat as directed by wisdom.

Schools must avoid levels 1 and 2, and should instead invite students to dine at a gourmet buffet that features a variety of intellectual, emotional, and social delicacies. The buffet should nourish students' determination and willpower to confront and overcome any stumbling blocks they may encounter. These delicacies provide students with the aptitudes, attitudes, and abilities they need to undertake life's challenges. Students should be fortified with the determination and the willful power not only to confront, but to overcome, any stumbling blocks they may encounter. Every day schools should initiate, nurture, and provide an innovative, authentic cuisine for the heart and mind of students. Schools must consistently foster students' insatiable appetite for knowledge. While there is no fool-proof recipe for alleviating school problems and issues, we can hope, believe, and strive to provide better learning opportunities for students.

Teachers Make a Difference

Teachers are pivotal to student success. While administrators, parents, and other stakeholders play a pertinent role in ensuring that students receive the best educational experiences possible, teachers are the most accountable, because they spend a great deal of contact time with students during the instructional day. Numerous research studies (e.g., Palmer, 1998), professional observations, and interviews indicate the enormous influence and impact that teachers have in tapping their students' potential and bringing out their students' best abilities.

Promoting Conation in the Classroom

If teachers wish to ensure their students' success, they must create conative classrooms. Conative classrooms use life-oriented experiences to create meaning, foster learning, and increase social wellness. Students learn how to make informed decisions and how to become productive citizens.

What Is It That Enables a Person to Act?

Students cannot truly do their best when they are feeling weak, incompetent, or alienated. If we expect learners to produce authentic results, then learners must feel a sense of ownership in their learning. Therefore, it is our job to help students feel strong, capable, and committed. Trust and confidence play a significant role in learning. Without trust and confidence, many students choose not to take risks. Without taking risks, students will not change. Without change, students will not grow.

Figure 3.2 illustrates the differences between a conative classroom and a non–conative classroom. The practices that can facilitate learning in the conative domain and strengthen bonds between students and intended goals are shown in Figure 3.3.

Conative Versus Non-Conative Classrooms

Characteristics of Conative Classrooms

- Students are actively engaged and take ownership of their learning.
- Teachers and students share mutual respect and joy.

- Collaboration is part of instruction.

- The classroom is a caring learning community.
- Independence and interdependence are communicated and experienced daily.

- Learning is appropriately rigorous and always supportive.

- Students know and use the conative power within themselves to make wise choices.
- Students can be seen giving their best inside and outside the classroom.

- Students feel and express a genuine sense of belonging.
- Teachers know their students and are open and accepting of all learners. They make the classroom an inviting place.

- Teachers believe that students have varied strengths and can all strive.

- Students believe in themselves and put forth effort to learn, while their teachers encourage them to establish and maintain personal standards of excellence.

Characteristics of Non-Conative Classrooms

- Students are disengaged and disinterested in learning.
- Teachers and students don't enjoy being in the classroom together and look forward to the end of the day.
- Instructional autonomy is the rule. There's only one way—the teacher's way.
- The classroom is a cold, unaccommodating, and uncaring environment.
- Independence and interdependence are discouraged. Students are asked to simply do what they are told.
- Learning is inappropriately rigorous or lacking in structure, substance, standards, or purpose.
- Students show lackluster performance, make poor choices, and are unfocused and apathetic.
- Students can be seen demonstrating inappropriate behavior inside and outside the classroom.
- Students feel and express a sense of alienation and rejection.
- Teachers are rigid and lack interest in some students' needs while showing favoritism toward others. They make the classroom a "disinviting" place.
- Teachers believe it is the students' job to pay attention and learn, whether or not teachers provide differentiated learning.
- Students fail to believe in themselves, put forth little effort to learn, and are angry and frustrated, while their teachers fail to encourage them to establish and maintain personal standards of excellence.

Figure 3.2

Teacher Actions That Promote Student Resilience

- **R**ecognize special gifts and talents of students, even if there is no place to show them on the report card.
- **E**mpower students by helping them to succeed in at least one small way each day.
- **S**mile when you see your students.
- **I**f you do not like something a student has done, help the individual understand that you still value him or her as a person.
- **L**isten (be fully present) when your students speak.
- **I**gnite the will to learn by seeking to know students beyond the façade they wear.
- **E**ncourage students to aim high.
- **N**urture excellence by inviting students to experience your excellence.
- **C**all students by their names.
- **E**nlighten students' view of what they can become and they will seek to give to you and the world the best of who they are.

Figure 3.3

Teachers seeking to develop their craft to the fullest view conation as a tool, a process, and a measure for gaining insight into when it is best to guide students, when to step back and allow them to move forward on their own, and when to "push" them (Borkowski et al., 1989; Dole et al., 1991; Paris & Winograd, 1990). The conative domain can forge connections between students and the goal, between opportunities and preparation, between inner strength and emotional intelligence, between challenge and stamina, between seeing the bigger picture and working toward that end, between belief in oneself and launching new ideas. Within the conative domain, we learn to give up on giving up, we trade in negative self-talk for breakthrough thinking and living, and we meet challenges with persistence and renewed energy (Gholar et al., 1991).

Connecting to Students' Lives Outside of School

Parents' love and care provide the best start for children in becoming loving and caring people. Simple gestures seem like big celebrations to children. Smiles, hugs, and kind words help to cultivate personal integrity and character. Parents who care enough to take a moment from their busy schedules to play, pause, listen, or simply laugh say to their children, "You are special, and someone special cares for you!" Being an integral part of a child's life gives both the adult and the young person permission to experience life in the moment. Bonds between parent and child that are grounded in a warm, nurturing environment build special relationships. In these relationships it is often difficult to tell which admires the other more. A child's inborn sense of wonder needs the companionship of at least one person who can share it.

Adults can encourage children to hope and dream by sharing their own hopes and aspirations with children. Parent-child relationships enable children to connect their dreams to self-confident, thoughtful actions. Healthy communication is key to developing a healthy self-image. Children desire to partake of life's fullness when they experience personal interactions that include vision, knowledge, and compassion.

"The way schools care about children is reflected in the way schools care about student families" (Epstein, 1995, p. 701). Students' families (or other external support systems) are an essential part of a student's success

A Bridge to Tomorrow

A teacher is a student's bridge to the future, a student's connection to the awesome. A teacher's power is in his or her knowledge, caring, belief, hope, energy, and presence.

in life and in school. However, engaging families in the learning process can be challenging. When parents have experienced negative situations in their own school careers, they may feel uncomfortable or even combative when they speak with teachers. Try meeting at a neutral location or communicating through telephone calls, notes, or e-mail messages. Share positive news about students and offer constructive, "do-able" strategies that parents can implement to increase students' success (Barr & Parrett, 2003).

Ensuring the Academic Success of Adolescents

In 1977, Lispsitz conducted a classic study subtitled *A Review of Research and Programs Concerning Early Adolescence.* This study focused attention on early adolescence—a unique stage of human development. Subsequent studies (McCombs & Whisler, 1989; Sizer, 1984) have indicated that young people between the ages of ten and fifteen face many challenges due to changes in their physical, social, emotional, mental, and moral development. "No other age level is of more importance to the future of individuals, and, literally, to that of society; because these are the years when youngsters crystallize their beliefs about themselves and firm up their self-concepts, their philosophies of life, and their values— the things that are the ultimate determinants of their behavior" (Lounsbury, 1996).

Talk to each other and learn in the process.

Those of us who interact with adolescents on a regular basis know that many of the perceptions and beliefs attributed to them are generally stereotypical, negative, and even mythical. Figure 3.4: A Profile of Today's Adolescent points out the complex needs and characteristics of today's youth. Some general characteristics that have been ascribed to middle school students include the idea that they are "a composite of raging hormones, who are often confused about who they are, want to be, or should be. They have a difficult time accepting their physical and emotional transformations; often see themselves as unattractive, unaccepted, unappreciated, and even unloved. They want very much to 'fit in,' but frequently feel isolated by their peers, teachers, and family."

In addition to the changes adolescents typically face, some adolescents experience social and emotional trauma, display antisocial behaviors, and exhibit a lack of moral and value-based attitudes and actions. Of course, we know these characteristics do not apply to all adolescents; however, research demonstrates that this population is at risk for succumbing to these negative characteristics.

Most young adolescents are quite "normal," according to research data and personal observations. They have strong morals and core values that preclude their participation in premarital sex, indulgence in alcohol and drugs, or other unacceptable social behaviors. They travel down the road of puberty rather effortlessly, avoiding many of the ditches of despair and potholes of uncertainty and confusion about their self-identity and future. They are happy, humorous, trusting, adventuresome,

---

A Profile of Today's Adolescent

May Be . . .	Yet May . . .
Technologically "Savvy"	Lack skill to organize, evaluate, synthesize data
Multicultural, Multilingual	Feel stymied by the ideas and language of one's culture
Used to Fast Access	Lack motivation to persevere for task completion
Socially Active	Lack the skills for purposeful social interaction
Peer Oriented	Need assistance with interpersonal relationships
Intellectually Capable	Be unpracticed in higher cognitive thinking
Future Oriented	Lack the skills for self-management and regulation
Exposed to Experience	Struggle with moral and ethical decisions
Information-Rich	Be limited in opportunities to explore broader issues
Independent-Minded	Be personally vulnerable to peer and societal lure
College-Work-Bound	Be limited in practical knowledge

Figure 3.4

Dream Big!

Our challenge is to explore ways to strengthen light in the midst of shadow. We must build connections in order to promote positive changes in behavior. We must use practical strategies that lead to excellence in school, at home, in the community, and throughout life. Through the passion of the will, we pursue excellence. Through the pursuit of excellence we climb—lifting others, setting them free to live, hope, and find themselves. Together we learn to run with our dreams.

clever, smart, street-wise, challenging, and hopeful. According to Piaget (as cited in Gunning, 2000), young adolescents are also able to think abstractly and to reason hypothetically. (Piaget called this the formal-operational stage of cognitive development, which typically occurs between the ages of eleven and fifteen.)

Addressing Feelings of Isolation and Hopelessness

Too many students feel like they are outsiders at school. Unfortunately, these feelings of alienation and isolation often increase as students get older. The poem "I Wish You Could Feel My Rage!" vividly illustrates one high school student's feelings of alienation (see Figure 3.5).

Attending to the conative aspect of student learning can help mitigate students' feelings of hopelessness by offering students opportunities to experience success. When teachers and schools work together with parents and other caregivers to support students, student achievement and attitude can change for the better.

I Wish You Could Feel My Rage!

Oh how I wish you could feel my rage!
I breathe in deeply, close my eyes, in darkness I exhale and ask . . .
Why do I have this rage within me?

The pain . . .
It comes on slowly and fiercely explodes into a fiery tidal wave
of contention.

If only you knew how it feels to be an outcast among peers
for no reason . . .
No future ahead—and nothing behind.

The emptiness, the loneliness
Wanting to be a part of something more
Rejected . . .

Made to feel useless—no purpose for living
Entombed and dead before I die
I wish you could feel my rage!

—HIGH SCHOOL STUDENT

Figure 3.5

Models of Perseverance

As early as preschool, children hear the fable of the tortoise and the hare and discover that the slow tortoise persevered to beat the hare in a seemingly impossible race. They also marvel at *The Little Engine That Could* (Piper, 1991). Each time the train engine says, "I think I can, I think I can," it puts forth more effort into climbing the mountain and it eventually succeeds! Children also watch and cheer *The Lion King* (Allers et al., 1994) and similar movies that portray courage, convictions, and the belief in one's self and one's ability.

As students grow, they begin to read about real people such as the Wright brothers, Harriet Tubman, Helen Keller, Jackie Robinson, and Anne Frank. Through *The Wright Brothers: How They Invented the Airplane* (Freeman, 1991), students learn that even though many others had failed and even died trying to attempt to fly, the Wright brothers were not deterred from their quest to fly. They experienced failure in their early attempts, but did not give up. They were self-motivated, had the will to succeed, and continuously put forth the effort needed to succeed in

Through a Child's Eyes

Children help us escape from the busyness of our day-to-day routines, and enter a place called "right here, and right now." Children are experts at living in the present moment. Through word and deed, we can tangibly communicate values that nurture respect, responsibility, and self-discipline. By setting a standard of excellence, we can strengthen our students' courage to cope responsibly in challenging situations. Children teach us courage not only to do something new, but to become someone new. Children allow themselves to be captivated by sights and sounds and uniquely weave these senses into the innocent way they see the world. We have a remarkable opportunity to provide them with a guiding companionship that will aid them as they begin to explore and navigate the waters of new and exciting experiences.

getting a plane to fly. When students read about Harriet Tubman, they discover another person who had conation. She was determined to lead as many slaves as possible to freedom. Even the threat of capture or death did not deter her will or impede her efforts to succeed in her mission. Students are engrossed with *The Story of My Life* (Keller, 2003), because they are fascinated with Helen Keller's drive, will, determination, and successful struggle to surmount what many would consider insurmountable obstacles. Stories about Jackie Robinson (e.g., *Jackie Robinson: Pro Ball's First Black Star* [Olsen, 1974]) also captivate students' attention as they discover how he fought discrimination and extreme racial prejudices to become America's first black major league baseball player. Jackie Robinson's story is yet another stellar example of pure drive, will,

Lessons Learned in Light and Shadow

The events of childhood linger long after the wonder and wisdom are gone. Lessons learned in shadow and in light often repeat themselves in the generations that follow. Our relationships with children affect the character and resilience of these children and of future generations. Through teaching, we not only affect the children before us, but we also influence our nation's intellectual, economic, social, and ethical future. How will the experiences of our students impact on what they will become? What will their experiences say about who we are? Are we instilling in them the fundamental core knowledge, beliefs, and values from which they can build their lives? What are we giving them to build upon? Stop, look, and listen to the lives of children.

courage, and determination that inspires students of all ethnic and cultural heritages. In *Anne Frank: The Diary of a Young Girl* (1956), students find themselves vicariously enduring the fear and ordeals faced by Anne, her family, and her friends. They also come to admire these people's tenacious will to survive and live in the midst of such cognitive dissonance. The life stories of people such as Winston Churchill, Tecumseh, Dr. Severo Ochoa, Cesar Chavez, and Nelson Mandela are other examples of individuals who persevered by sheer will, determination, and effort.

> **Survey the infrastructure of the will and define what success means for each student.**

The sample lessons at the end of this chapter acquaint students with stories of perseverance. The lessons motivate students to establish and reach for their own goals so that they might better understand the concept of conation.

The Origins of Success and Failure

Our nation needs productive students and resilient teachers who are prepared and committed to give their personal and professional best. Meeting the needs of *all* learners involves instructional leadership—leadership that transforms and differentiates instruction in order to increase academic achievement. The conative domain provides an access route for building greater collaboration and deeper engagement in the process of learning. Teachers can foster the underlying thinking needed to positively influence students' academic and social behavior, while laying the groundwork that ensures that students are interested in what they are being taught.

Teachers who focus on conation also seek to enhance students' problem-solving and question-posing skills. In this process, the teacher's role becomes more and more transparent. That is, the teacher refrains from *delivering* lessons and instead shifts to *mentoring* students in finding and solving problems. In this role, the teacher becomes aware of the conative power of teachable moments. Teachable moments take students beyond the immediate lesson, drawing them into asking significant how and why questions (e.g., "How can I accomplish this?" and "Why is it important for me to learn this?"). Excellent teachers have the courage to extend themselves in order to bridge the gap between emerging understanding and complete understanding. When we keep conation in mind, we strengthen teacher–student relationships through consensus-building and support. As we become better mentors, students build self-knowledge, mental toughness, emotional resilience, and personal commitment.

We educators often hear the statement, "Start where they are." When we begin with conation in mind, we discover that students may not "start" where first anticipated. Some may be more advanced; others may need additional support. Some students may require a stronger and more positive union between self-perception and their willingness to try. Remember, schools serve students with tremendously diverse backgrounds and personal beliefs about learning. We must be prepared to provide students with multiple entry and exit points in the learning process. For example, we should

- acknowledge each student's growth and achievement, while maintaining focus on curriculum and instruction;
- support and encourage students to open themselves to learning without restrictions and to fully engage in the learning process; and
- hold high expectations for all learners, even those who appear to struggle or who are reluctant to learn.

If we keep conation in mind, we will know when to lead, when to gently push students, and when to let go, allowing learners to soar in varied and unique ways with their academic pursuits.

✸

Lessons from

the **Heart**
of **Learning**

We often hear the statement "if we don't learn from history, we are doomed or bound to repeat it." This concept is lost on too many of our young people because they live and learn just for the present. There is a great deal to be learned from real and fictional events about ethical behavior, treatment of our fellow man, our individual values and beliefs, and the crucial role of the will in the struggle for survival, existence, and "the good life."

The following lessons have been designed to motivate students' interest in and knowledge of events in history, as well as fictional accounts, that have inspired some individuals to willfully perform feats of unselfishness, bravery, and compassion; or events that provoked others to use their gift of determination and perseverance to engage in undesirable and detrimental activities. These lessons challenge students to reflect on their actions, motives, beliefs, and values and, hopefully, gain a better understanding of ethical behavior.

(Note: To learn how to design lessons that reach the heart of learning, see chapter 4.)

Am I My Brother's Keeper?

I expect to pass through life but once. If therefore, there be any kindness I can show, or any good thing I can do to any fellow human being, let me do it now, and not defer or neglect it, as I shall not pass this way again.—WILLIAM PENN, 1644

WHAT'S IT ALL ABOUT?

Purpose

* To acquaint students with historical events that impacted millions of lives
* To promote a better understanding of discrimination and intolerance
* To help students discover how one person's courageous voice, actions, and care can make a difference
* To help students understand that "people are people" regardless of culture, religion, or ethnicity
* To have students recognize that all human life has value and worth

Instructional Objectives

* Students will develop an appreciation for and understanding of historical events.
* Students will improve their comprehension and critical thinking skills.
* Students will enhance their knowledge and understanding of characterization in nonfiction genres.
* Students will explore the concept of "man's inhumanity to man."
* Students will explore cognitive, affective, and conative behaviors via various historical events.
* Students will examine the power of metaconation in ethical decision making.

Interdisciplinary Implementation

* History
* Language arts
* Library science
* Career education
* Technology

Instructional Focus

Students will read "Stranger on the Bus" and reflect on the following:

- research methodology;
- reading, writing, and thinking; and
- metacognition.

MAKING THE CONNECTION

Instructional Strategies and Activities

1. Encourage students to read "Stranger on the Bus."
2. Divide students into cooperative groups of three to five students.
3. Ask students to answer the following questions (in their groups or as a whole class):
   - Why do you think the man came to the rescue of the Jewish woman?
   - Why do you think he risked his life to help this woman?
   - Would you consider him courageous, brave, and sympathetic? Give reasons and examples for your response.
   - Do you think you would have or could have acted in the same manner had you been this man? Why or why not?
   - What kind of person would he have to be to do what he did?
   - Why do you think there was so much hatred for Jews?
   - Why do you think there is still hatred, resentment, and discrimination against certain ethnic groups in this, the twenty-first century?
4. Discuss students' answers to the questions. Use students' answers to motivate them to complete the research project (see Extended Research).

CONATIVE HOOK: Now that I *know*, what will I *do*?

Extended Research and Reflection

1. Challenge teams to conduct research about this period of history. Explain that they should use historical texts, the Internet, and other resources to learn about and acquaint themselves with this period. Tell students to read historical stories (e.g., *Anne Frank: Diary of a Young Girl*) or watch movies (e.g., *Schindler's List, The Pianist*) that depict the horrors of the Holocaust.

2. Ask students to examine, discuss, and note significant events such as the rise of Hitler, the growing resentment of and discrimination toward the Jewish population, the establishment of the death camps, etc.

3. Challenge each team to select one or more of these events to research. Explain that the team should compile its findings by writing a collective research paper.

4. Encourage teams to share their papers with the class.

Stranger on the Bus
by Lawrence Kushner

A light snow was falling and the streets were crowded with people. It was Munich in Nazi Germany. One of my rabbinic students, Shifra Penzias, told me her great-aunt, Sussie, had been riding a city bus home from work when SS storm troopers suddenly stopped the coach and began examining the identification papers of the passengers. Most were annoyed but a few were terrified. Jews were being told to leave the bus and get into a truck around the corner.

My student's great-aunt watched from her seat in the rear as the soldiers systematically worked their way down the aisle. She began to tremble, tears streaming down her face. When the man next to her noticed she was crying, he politely asked her why.

"I don't have the papers you have. I am a Jew. They're going to take me."

The man exploded with disgust. He began to curse and scream at her. "You stupid [woman]," he roared. "I can't stand being near you!"

The SS men asked what all the yelling was about.

"Damn her," the man shouted angrily. "My wife has forgotten her papers again! I'm so fed up. She always does this!"

The soldiers laughed and moved on.

My student said that her great-aunt never saw the man again. She never even knew his name.

Ask students to reflect upon the following questions:
- Have you acquired a better understanding of this period in history? What have you learned?
- Have you heard of, read about, or watched movies that depict the cruelty of humans against fellow humans (man's inhumanity to man)? For example, have you heard about the poor treatment of Chinese people, the cruelties of slavery, and the interment of Japanese-Americans?
- Have any of your previous concepts, biases, or misconceptions about certain cultures or ethnic groups changed? (Note: If students feel uncomfortable, they need not answer this question aloud. Rather, encourage them to reflect on the question privately.)

ASSESSMENT

Assess the success of the lesson by asking yourself the following questions:
1. Did students gain a new body of knowledge about historical events, events that included discrimination and prejudice? How did they demonstrate this knowledge?
2. How effectively did students apply their metacognitive, literacy, and critical thinking skills? How was this evidenced?
3. Were students able to understand the underlying theme (how individuals and groups are able to persevere and survive under impossible odds and conditions)? How was this evidenced by each student?

Does the End Justify the Means?

What lies behind us and what lies before us are tiny matters compared to what lies within us.—RALPH WALDO EMERSON

WHAT'S IT ALL ABOUT?

Purpose
- To acquaint students with the elements of fictional stories
- To develop an awareness of ethical values and positive character traits
- To promote an understanding of intrinsic motivation
- To emphasize the importance of moral decisions
- To help students understand the power of the will

Instructional Objectives
- Students will develop an understanding of caring, responsibility, honesty, and courage and how these traits impact one's life.
- Students will develop a knowledge and understanding of narrative, expository, descriptive, and persuasive writing.
- Students will explore their creative writing abilities.
- Students will enhance their inference, critical thinking, and comprehension skills.
- Students will examine moral issues and will discuss whether or not particular situations justify illegal actions.

Interdisciplinary Implementation
- Language arts
- Library science
- Science
- Character education

Instructional Focus

Students will read "The Story of Jack and the Beanstalk" and will
- Be able to relate fiction with real life incidents in determining values
- Be able to recognize and determine ethical issues dealing with right vs. wrong
- Be able to use fictional narrative to develop and/or enhance skills in creative writing, inferring, comprehending, and distinguishing the various writing discourses

MAKING THE CONNECTION

Instructional Strategies and Activities

Part 1: Writing Activities
1. Divide students into cooperative teams of three to five students. Ask teams to read the retold version of "Jack and the Beanstalk."
2. Challenge teams to complete the writing activities at the end of the story.
3. Encourage teams to share their writing with the other teams. Discuss the presentations. Then compare the presentations and select the most original and creative responses.

Part 2: Jack—A Hero or a Criminal?
4. Place students in three cooperative teams for a debate. Explain each team's role:
   a. Team A will take the pro position: Jack was justified in going into the giant's castle, taking advantage of his unhappy wife, and stealing his possessions. This team will argue the case that Jack had conative qualities, that he was brave, strong-minded, and persistent in his endeavors to provide for his mother and himself. Team A will also argue that the giant's death was accidental and he deserved to die. Team A will be in favor of declaring Jack a hero, who exhibited bravery, tenacity, and responsibility for his actions.

b. Team B will take the con position (the opposite position from Team A): Jack was a common thief and murderer, in spite of his dire circumstances. It will contend that Jack was not an acceptable role model for exhibiting perseverance or determination just because he continued to return to the castle in spite of the danger of being discovered. This team will be opposed to attributing any positive characteristics to Jack or his actions. Jack will be portrayed as dishonest, conniving, lazy, and a murderous thief. This team will address the ethical dilemma of whether or not "the end justified the means."

c. Team C will act as a panel of adjudicators. Members of this team will listen to the rationale, arguments, and justifications presented by Team A and Team B, and then determine which team best supported its pro or con position. Team C may use the Debate Scoring Sheet to record points earned by Team A and Team B.

5. Hold the debate. Ask Team C to determine which team made the best argument.

CONATIVE HOOK: Now that I *know*, what will I *do*?

Extended Research and Reflection

Encourage students to consider how they might have handled:

a. selling the cow?

b. making (or not making) trips up the beanstalk?

c. the incident with the giant?

ASSESSMENT

Assess the success of the lesson by asking yourself the following questions:

1. Did students exhibit a knowledge of conventional writing skills and the writing process? How?

2. How did students demonstrate their understanding of fictional characters and fictional incidents in the story?

3. Were students able to identify and understand the underlying themes of responsibility, dishonesty, bravery, and determination? How was this demonstrated by each student?

4. Do students know and understand the tenets of narrative, expository, persuasive, and descriptive writing? How did students exhibit this knowledge and understanding?

5. Were students able to understand the difference between ethical and unethical actions? How was this demonstrated?

The Story of Jack and the Beanstalk
Retold by Ernestine Riggs

Once upon a time there lived, in a very poor town, a boy named Jack and his mother. Now Jack was not the brightest boy, but he had a good disposition, told great jokes, and was kind and loving. He was, however, extremely lazy. Some attributed his laziness to the fact that he was "brain challenged." Jack's mother, like most mothers, loved her son, but knew he had a few cards missing from the deck.

One day, after the mother had given Jack the last piece of bread in the house, she looked around and realized she had sold every possible possession they had in the world in her effort to feed herself and her son. All they had left of any value was the old, dried-out cow. So she gave Jack the responsibility of taking their last food source to town to sell.

She explained to Jack the importance of getting the highest possible price for the cow. The more money he was able to get, the more food they could buy, and the longer they would be able to survive. Happy that his mother trusted him with this significant task, Jack set off for town with the old cow. He had not gotten very far before he encountered a strange looking little individual who, after talking to Jack for a few minutes, knew Jack was an easy mark. He talked Jack into trading the cow for five pretty beans. Jack ran home, proud and excited, thinking he had made a great deal. Of course you know what his mother thought! She was so angry that she threw the beans out of the window, where they landed in the back yard. She sent Jack to bed hungry.

Well, the next day when Jack woke up, to his great surprise, he found a gigantic beanstalk had grown from the beans his mother had thrown out of the window. Like most boys he was curious, so he climbed up the beanstalk and stepped into a strange and different land. After checking out his surroundings, he spied a castle down the road. He approached the castle cautiously, walked up to the huge doors, knocked timidly, and asked for some food.

It so happened the castle belonged to a "cannibal giant." Luckily for Jack, the giant's wife came to the door. She informed him of the giant's fondness for "people stew" and begged him to leave. But Jack sweet-talked her into letting him in the house, whereby she fed him a delicious vegetarian meal.

Now the giant's wife had been married, as far as she was concerned, much too long. In fact, she was really tired of the bulky, repulsive, gluttonous giant and longed to be free and single again. When the giant returned home unexpectedly early, she hid Jack in the oven where he remained until the giant fell asleep. When Jack was sure the giant was sleeping soundly, he stole the hen that produced golden eggs and ran home via the beanstalk. He and his mother lived quite well until the hen ceased laying the golden eggs. This turn of events created the need for another trip up the beanstalk.

Jack again convinced the wife to allow him entrance into the castle, where he proceeded to rummage around until he found a golden harp. However, when he attempted its theft, it played a "help me" song which woke the giant, causing Jack to run for his life. The giant tried to follow Jack down the beanstalk, but Jack managed to get down first, grab an ax, and chop down the stalk with the giant swaying on it. Needless to say, the big guy was killed.

Jack and his mother, concerned about the legal consequences of the incident, went to the town's psychic, who assured them they would live rich and happy lives forever and ever.

Writing Activities

1. You are a reporter for your local newspaper and you have been given the assignment of interviewing the giant's wife after the giant's death. Create five significant questions you will ask her as you attempt to discover what really happened. Imagine how she might answer the questions and write about her version of the incident. (Narrative)

2. Using your prior knowledge about plants and their growth cycle, create a fictional bean and a scientific explanation for the type of beans Jack obtained from the stranger. Base your explanation on real scientific facts about plants. (Expository)

3. Jack was eventually caught and charged with breaking, entering, and murder. You are his attorney. You must convince the jury that Jack is innocent of all charges. You must gather evidence (create this evidence), interview witnesses (make up interviews), and write your findings for presentation to the jury. How will you convince the jury that what Jack did was not wrong and that he is innocent? (Persuasive)

4. In your summation (as Jack's lawyer), one strategy you will use is to create as much sympathy and empathy for your client as possible. Therefore, you must paint a graphic picture, with explicit and descriptive details and examples about Jack's environment (e.g., his single-parent home, his neighborhood, his mother's lack of parenting skills, etc.). Create a description that will bring the jurors to tears. (Descriptive and Creative)

Debate Scoring Sheet

Team A: Pro

Characteristics

1.

2.

3.

4.

Behavior

1.

2.

3.

4.

Rationale for Behavior

1.

2.

3.

4.

Comments (by Team C):

Team B: Con

Characteristics

1.

2.

3.

4.

Behavior

1.

2.

3.

4.

Rationale for Behavior

1.

2.

3.

4.

Comments (by Team C):

Jack—A Hero or a Criminal?
Rubric for Evaluating Debate

Directions: Determine the number of points each team earns on each on the skills listed below. Check the appropriate numerical box using the key guide. Total the ten features. Highest possible points = 50.

Key: 5 = Exceptionally effective; 4 = Highly effective; 3 = Proficiently effective; 2 = Slightly effective; 1 = Absolutely ineffective

Presentation/Organization	Team A					Team B				
	5	4	3	2	1	5	4	3	2	1
1. Spoke clearly, used correct sentence structure and appropriate, fluent, and creative vocabulary										
2. Used effective verbal and nonverbal communication (voice quality, body language, eye contact)										
3. Answered questions with details and examples										
4. Addressed the issue effectively, to the point, and in a sincere manner										
5. Exhibited respect and demonstrated appreciation for others' viewpoints										
6. Presented viewpoints in an organized and logical manner										
7. Provided justification for answers, comments, and conclusions										
8. Maintained focus on the topic; delivery of ideas connected logically										
9. Presented characters, their values, beliefs, attributes, character traits, and personalities in an inspired, creative, and thought-provoking manner										
10. Convinced jury (Team C) of the validity of points of view presented; persuaded and won the sentiment and votes of this panel										

Total for Team A:____   Total for Team B:____

FURTHER READING

Allington, R. L., & Cunningham, P. M. (2002). *Schools that work: Where all children read and write* (2nd ed.). Boston: Allyn and Bacon.

Banks, J. A. (1988). Ethnicity, class, cognitive, and motivational styles: Research and teaching implications. *Journal of Negro Education, 57*(4), 452–466.

Barr, R., & Parrett, W. (2003). *Saving our students, saving our schools: 50 proven strategies for revitalizing at-risk students and low-performing schools.* Glenview, IL: Pearson Professional Development.

Beamon, G. (2001). *Teaching with adolescent learning in mind.* Arlington Heights, IL: SkyLight Professional Development.

Gunning, T. (2000). *Creating literacy instruction for all children.* Boston: Allyn and Bacon.

Haycock, K. (1998). *Good teaching matters.* Washington, DC: Education Trust.

Kohl, H. (1991). *I won't learn from you!: The role of assent in learning.* Minneapolis: Milkweed.

Purkey, W. W., & Novak, J. M. (1986). *Inviting school success: A self-concept approach to teaching, learning, and democratic practice* (3rd ed.). Belmont, CA: Wadsworth.

CHAPTER

4

Captivate, Connect, and Cultivate

Student

Success doesn't always mean that you have to be at the top of the class. For me it means **understanding what you have to do.** When I understand the task that is before me, I do it. There are many times that I need help and I ask for it. **My mom, my teacher, and my friends and I work together. They are not afraid** to stop me if my work is incorrect. **I ask a lot of questions and I try. I do my best to keep up. My grades are getting better. Always ask for help and you'll get it.**

—ELEMENTARY STUDENT

Teacher

Every child is capable of learning. If a teacher is not getting through to a child, **then it is the teacher's responsibility to find a way to get the child to learn**—make the light bulb go on.

—ELEMENTARY TEACHER

Conative Strategies for Engaging Learners

Why is conation important to the learning process? Conation transforms ability into action—the process we use to fulfill our goals (Kolbe, 1990). Motivation sets the stage for action and conation carries out the action (Corno & Kanfer, 1993). The conative domain connects to new adventures in learning. It provides a construct or model for teaching students new concepts (see Figure 4.1).

This chapter provides a variety of strategies and activities based on the concept of conation (the *will, determination,* and *internal drive* to succeed). These activities have been designed to empower students' sense of well being and rekindle their hearts with a commitment of becoming the best they can be. The activities help students thoroughly examine their beliefs about who they are and about what they can achieve. The goal of each activity is to address a holistic approach to teaching and learning. The activities blend the conative, cognitive, and affective domains in an integrative and cohesive manner. The activities will help students become aware of their own conative abilities, improve their cognitive skills (literacy and critical thinking), and enhance their affective (emotional) development.

The Three C's of Conation

- **Captivate:** Seize students' attention with interesting, grade- and subject-appropriate materials and authentic tasks.

- **Cultivate:** Foster and encourage the development and refinement of students' abilities, skills, gifts, and talents.

- **Connect:** Establish a bridge between what is taught and what is learned.

(Adapted from Hixson, Gholar, & Riggs, 1999.)

Figure 4.1

First, Dream

In the conative domain, the learner engages his action and will to produce academic persistence. The purposeful desire to strive and the determination to acquire knowledge or a skill are critical to student achievement and authentic success. Students with conation are ready to accomplish a task. If conation is infused into the synergy of learning, the result will be a self-motivated, competent, knowledgeable, and productive learner.

In the conative domain, a teacher's attempt to facilitate learning becomes actualized through the individual student's **will**, **drive**, and **effort** to achieve. Learning is transformed into the acquisition of knowledge. Conation sets in motion the charge to learn and the responsibility to carry out that charge. In moments of internal conflict, the charge to excel will overpower the temptation to procrastinate in completing the task at hand, or to ignore it altogether. Conation tackles every obstacle, carries the learner forward, and propels the student to achieve or surpass the intended goal. Conative learners take charge of their learning. Through persistence, the learner transforms potential into reality.

Teachers not only have the power to help students achieve their dreams, they can also help students discover their dreams. Teachers can encourage students to ascertain what gives them enjoyment, to find harmony in their lives and environment, to determine a sense of purpose, and to discover their own conative capacity (internal drive). If students own these ideas, they are better equipped to cope with life's challenges, disappointments, and other obstacles.

Designing Lessons That Reach the Heart of Learning

Research has indicated that students learn more effectively when they are more actively engaged in their own learning (Wolfe, 2001). Therefore, conative lessons must be active. Conative lessons must also be

- personally relevant;
- appropriate (to students' developmental level);
- authentic (intellectually intriguing);
- challenging yet safe (without fear or potential for embarrassment);
- collaborative;
- flexible (providing students a number of ways to demonstrate learning); and
- adaptable (offering appropriate options).

The lessons that appear at the end of every chapter are exemplars of conative instructional design. Each lesson begins with a quotation by a famous person. The quotation can be used to engage the learner. Each lesson also includes the following:

- Purpose
- Instructional Objectives
- Interdisciplinary Implementation
- Instructional Focus
- Instructional Strategies and Activities
- Extended Research
- Reflections
- Assessment

Each of the elements is described in the following paragraphs.

What's It All About?

Purpose. Conative learning begins when the teacher and learners know why they are engaging in a particular activity and how the activity will improve conation. Be sure to identify at least three purposes for each lesson. An example of a purpose is "To promote one's understanding of his or her own ability to achieve a desired goal."

Instructional Objectives. These statements describe observable behaviors and actions that students should be able to do by the end of the lesson. Remember to align these objectives with your state and district standards.

Interdisciplinary Implementation. Research shows that learners benefit when learning standards from different content areas that are combined within the same lesson or unit (Ellis & Fouts, 1997; Jensen, 2001; Shanahan & Newman, 1997). Providing interdisciplinary activities

- helps learners discover and connect concepts,
- increases the learners' motivation (will to learn), and
- helps teachers manage an overloaded curriculum.

Authentic action for authentic learning leads to academic accountability, self-respect, and high performance.

Instructional Focus. This section identifies the content that will be taught. We recommend using the life stories of real people. Examining the lives of other people helps students examine their own lives and to find personal meaning in their learning.

Making the Connection

Instructional Strategies and Activities. This section describes the step-by-step process used in the lesson. See Using Teaching Strategies Effectively in the Conative Domain for learning strategies you can use to develop this section of the lesson.

Conative Hook: Now That I *Know*, What Will I *Do*?

Extended Research and Reflection. This section should provide direction for further student research on the lesson topic. One way to know if a student has begun to work within the conative domain is if she wants to learn more about a given topic. Students should be given opportunities to explore the lesson topic outside of the lesson plan.

During the reflection stage of the lesson, students are given an opportunity to think more about what they have learned. Without metacognitive time, true learning cannot occur. Use open-ended questions to facilitate reflection.

Assessment

The Fifth Discipline Fieldbook asserts that "change and learning may not exactly be synonymous, but they are inextricably linked" (Senge et al., 1994). Any assessment plan should provide varied opportunities for students to exhibit how they have changed. Conation is about change. In addition, teachers should assess the power of their lessons to bring about change and refine their lessons to increase their effectiveness.

Using Teaching Strategies Effectively in the Conative Domain

The strategies that follow are, for the most part, open-ended or non-prescriptive. Therefore, they provide students with opportunities to construct meaning and connect to their prior knowledge and experiences. When these strategies are constructively woven into lessons, students are able to make conative connections to the lesson topic and thereby enjoy positive learning experience that will stay with them.

Anticipation Guides

Anticipation guides, as the name infers, help students make predictions. Anticipation guides usually include four to ten stereotypical or controversial statements. The statements are usually written in a yes-no, agree-disagree, or true-false format. Students read each statement and draw conclusions based on what they know, what they think they know, or what they can guess before they read a selection or learn about a new topic. After students complete the anticipation guide, they read the text or learn about the topic in order to determine how accurate their predictions were. Some sample anticipation guides are shown in Figure 4.2.

Sample Anticipation Guides

Primary Example
Anticipation Guide for *How the Sea Became Salt*
Circle Yes if you think the answer is correct. Circle No if you think the answer is not correct.

Yes	No	1. This story is about a sea who wanted to be salt.
Yes	No	2. Everyone loves the taste of salt.
Yes	No	3. Salt is good for you.
Yes	No	4. This is a true story.

Intermediate/Middle School Example
Anticipation Guide for *The Witness (Ash-Shahid)*
If you agree with the statement, circle Agree. If you disagree with the statement, circle Disagree.

Agree	Disagree	1. This story is about someone who is a witness to a crime.
Agree	Disagree	2. Ash-Shahid is the witness
Agree	Disagree	3. Ash-Shahid is not an American.
Agree	Disagree	4. This story is not about a crime.
Agree	Disagree	5. People who are witnesses always tell the truth.
Agree	Disagree	6. Someone who is a foreigner cannot be a witness.
Agree	Disagree	7. Witnesses must swear to tell the truth or they go to jail.
Agree	Disagree	8. Children cannot be a witness.

High School Example
Anticipation Guide for *The Topic of Graphs*
If you think the statement is correct, circle True. If you think the statement is incorrect, circle False.

True	False	1. Everyone is smart in math.
True	False	2. Graphs are charts that show comparisons.
True	False	3. Graphs can always be used to help you understand a problem.
True	False	4. Newspapers do not use graphs.
True	False	5. Students should be required to make graphs for problems they don't understand.
True	False	6. Only students who are good in art can make graphs.
True	False	7. Students who know how to do math should not have to make graphs.
True	False	8. Students in elementary school are not smart enough to understand graphs.
True	False	9. Bar graphs are the easiest to make and understand.
True	False	10. Students who cannot make good graphs are not smart.

Figure 4.2

Anticipation guides are designed to motivate students to

- Rely on their own metacognitive skills
- Evaluate the statements or issues based on their individual paradigms
- Access and use their prior knowledge to make sensible inferences
- Debate the issues without the restrictions or limitations of having "the right answer"

Using an anticipation guide in the conative domain provides each student with the opportunity to experience cognitive, affective, and conative success. Some teachers are not aware of the fact that many students have never experienced the joy or sense of accomplishment in knowing what it feels like to "have that right answer" or have their opinion accepted and valued, regardless of how far out of the box it may seem.

Using anticipation guides is one way to captivate, connect, and cultivate students' will to want to learn and participate in the process of learning and doing. Why? Because the student has a fighting chance of succeeding, of demonstrating that he has something to offer, and proving that he has a brain. These guides give each student (as well as the teacher) an opportunity to explore and discover their multiple intelligences. When students realize the threat of failure has been diminished or eliminated, they are more willing to take risks. They exhale the fear of disappointment, embarrassment, and degradation, and inhale the feeling of self-worth, achievement, and even triumph.

A Wellspring of Learning

Deep within each person is the conative domain—the will, drive, and determination to succeed. We can tap into a wellspring of learning, the heart of the matter, the place where fortitude, commitment, adaptability, and persistence are nurtured, if we educators have the will.

How many teachers have experienced that awesome moment when Timothy or Samantha discovered where to find the "switch" (in their own mind, will, and brain) and turned on the light ("I got it!"). When students are given the opportunity to become intentional inquirers and self-discovers and are able to experience success in this pursuit, they will likely become willing participants in the learning process.

> When the will to do good defines one's life, and when one's ethical expressions for living visibly celebrate the good in others . . . one experiences higher levels of knowing and being.

Graphic Organizers

Graphic organizers are visual representations. They are also referred to as

- visual organizers,
- semantic maps or webs,
- structured overviews, and
- mind maps.

Graphic organizers are mental tools that learners use to aid in their understanding and remembering. Research has indicated that a large percentage of students are visual learners. Therefore, graphic organizers are effective learning tools, because they include both visual images and words.

Research has proven that graphic organizers are one of the most effective instructional strategies in improving comprehension (Ogle, 2000). They are instructionally "universal"; that is, they can be used with any subject, content area, and grade level. They are also effective with all types of students—from the gifted to those with special needs (Lehman et al., 1992; Sorenson, 1991). They promote vocabulary development (Toms-Bronowski, 1983).

There are many types of graphic organizers. Following is an explanation of two of the most frequently used graphic organizers and how they may be used to enhance instruction.

Semantic Webs. These graphic organizers help learners discover and create connections between ideas. Students are usually given a topic and are asked to brainstorm ideas connected to the given topic.

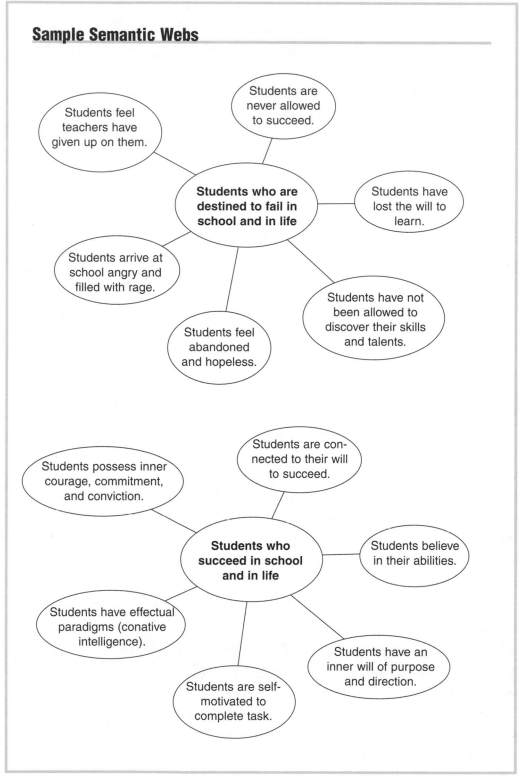

Figure 4.3

The semantic webs shown in Figure 4.3 show some brainstormed ideas about the causes of failure and the causes of success in school and in life. You may use the blackline master in Figure 4.4 to practice creating a semantic web. Use the blackline on your own or adapt it for use with your students.

Semantic Web for Examining Your Values

1. Use the semantic web to the right to brainstorm all the things that you believe would enrich your life or make you happy if you had money to buy them.

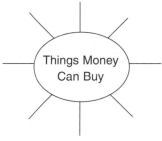

2. Select four items from your web and answer the following questions in one or two short paragraphs:
   - How did you narrow your list to these four items?
   - Why do you feel or think these things could enrich your life or make you happy?
   - How do you plan to obtain the money that will enable you to buy all of the things your heart desires?

3. Use the semantic web to the right to brainstorm all the things that would enrich your life that money *cannot* buy.

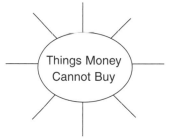

4. Select four items from your web and answer the following questions in one or two short paragraphs:
   - How did you narrow your list to these four items?
   - Why do you feel or think these things could enrich your life or make you happy?
   - Why do you feel that money is not necessary to enrich your life or make you happy?

5. Compare your list with those of your peers and discuss your selections and reasons.

Figure 4.4

Semantic Feature Analysis (SFA). The semantic feature analysis (SFA) graphic organizer provides students with a visual technique to simply and effectively compare the characteristics of different ideas, objects, concepts, views, or beliefs. SFAs help students comprehend and learn required material. In turn, students gain an effective tool for overcoming instructional challenges and succeeding in learning required material. An example SFA is shown in Figure 4.5.

Sample Semantic Feature Analysis

(High School Level)
Know Your Leaders

Identify the people listed below according to their leadership style by placing an X in the appropriate box.

	Leader	President	Dictator	Religious Leader	Royalty	Other
Thomas Jefferson						
Louis XIV						
Mohandas Gandhi						
Ayatollah Khomeini						
Elizabeth I						
Genghis Khan						
Golda Meir						
Joan of Arc						
Eleanor Roosevelt						
Adolf Hitler						
Ivan the Terrible						
Winston Churchill						
Julius Caesar						
Nelson Mandela						

Figure 4.5

Increasing Student Self-Efficacy with Choice

As discussed in chapter 2, students must *choose* to learn. Choice is also an important factor when designing instruction in the conative domain. Teachers can nurture student self-direction and personal efficacy by providing students with choices prior to, during, and after lessons. This doesn't mean that students will make all the decisions, nor does it mean reverting to personal relevance curricula of the 1960s. When we emphasize student self-direction and efficacy, we use strategies that offer students opportunities to make decisions and solve problems on their own. Students learn to process information with confidence, come to believe that they have the ability to strive to succeed, begin to set their own goals for personal development and instructional improvement, and plan how they might achieve their goals. Perhaps most important, students become more reflective about their thinking and what they are learning. "[W]hen students are working on goals they themselves have set, they are more motivated and efficient, and they achieve more than they do when working on goals that have been set by the teacher" (Hom & Murphy, 1983).

From the business world, we know that people who attain success are those who plan, identify goals, and design strategies to work toward those goals (Peters & Waterman, 1982). Likewise, students must learn a variety of problem-solving strategies in order to reach their goals. In order to solve complex problems, learners should learn to

- talk through the problem,
- ask what they know and what they need to find out,
- pose questions,
- visualize relationships using existing knowledge, and
- draw their own conclusions (Perkins, 1992; Pressley et al., 1992).

When we encourage students to develop awareness about their own thinking and learning, we also help them analyze the effectiveness of the strategies they choose to reach their goals. When students realize that their thoughts control their actions (i.e., that their locus of control is internal), they can positively affect their own beliefs and academic performance.

Achieving High Performance in Spite of the Odds

Without energy and will, high performance cannot be achieved. When we push beyond the façade of anger and emptiness that some reluctant learners express, we open ourselves and them to new possibilities and a future that perhaps they never would have known. People change when they feel they have hope. Is your classroom filled with hope? Is there anything that you can do to support the change you want to see in students who are not engaged in learning?

When we teach with conation in mind, we find that conation is its own reward. Conation enables learners to seek higher levels of learning while strengthening their courage and character. Actually, conation reveals who we truly are beneath the surface, and what we are truly made of in terms of energy, endurance, and fortitude.

The Passageway to Achievement

A person driven by the will to succeed travels on a journey to success. As the learner travels down the road, she will acquire battle scars while overcoming obstacles. However, the battle scars are merely evidence of the learner's intellectual heroism and courage. The learner comes to believe that she can transform current challenges into passageways that lead to achievement, because she receives encouragement from internal (her own conative spirit) and external (teachers, parents, significant others) sources.

Our efforts to transform learning into high performance begins with our understanding of what makes learning happen—what brings about the *will* to learn, what creates the "buy-in," and what transforms a life. In our search to define success in academics and in life, we know that some students simply need to uncover within themselves the will and determination to learn and "to do." Who will show them? Who will teach them? Who will be there for them? The answer is us! We teachers must be the leaders!

At the heart of learning, there's a human story.

Through conation, goals are accomplished, success is achieved, results are attained, and intellectual effort is put forth. Every individual has the ability to take action. However, ability remains in the form of potential until knowledge and emotions are moved into productive action.

The conative world is small, yet multidimensional. It is the world of the mind and heart filled with cheerleaders, constructivists, and instructional bulldozers, all doing their part to level the intellectual playing field and to cheer the learner on to academic success and greatness. The victorious cheers that come from *within* guide our students down the highway of fulfillment, purpose, and a meaningful life. We must teach our young people to be cognizant of the road signs, pay attention to the detours and barriers, but constantly remind and instill in them the fact that they have the *knowledge, will, determination,* and *power* to successfully reach their destination—if they put forth the effort.

✳

Lessons from

the **Heart** of **Learning**

Teachers, administrators, parents, and other stakeholders are aware of the fact that when a student has a sense of self–worth and confidence, they are better equipped to cope with academic and personal challenges that they are confronted with on a daily basis. They are able to deal with "uninviting" and sometimes hostile learning environments because they are aware of their intellectual strengths and have a firm belief in themselves, their values, and their abilities. However, some students may not be aware of their qualities until given the opportunity to reflect on and explore their inner essence.

The following lessons have been designed to help students think about their positive attributes, identify their strengths, recognize their abilities, and discover their individual skills, gifts, and talents. This process will help them to understand they have the power and inner ability to succeed.

Conative Character Map

Nothing in this world can take the place of persistence. Talent will not; nothing is more common than unsuccessful people with talent.—CALVIN COOLIDGE

WHAT'S IT ALL ABOUT?

Purpose

* To acquaint students with the elements of narrative and expository texts
* To develop an awareness of cultures, genders, and ethnicities through various characters and their traits
* To promote an understanding of the elements of character development through reading and writing activities
* To promote an understanding of one's ability to accomplish a desired goal in life
* To help students understand the power of the will

Instructional Objectives

* Students will develop an understanding of character traits and how these traits impact on one's life.
* Students will improve comprehension and critical thinking skills through an in-depth analysis of characters and their actions.
* Students will enhance their knowledge and understanding of characterization in fiction and nonfiction genres.
* Students will gain an understanding of cognitive, affective, and conative skills as they explore characters in various situations.

Interdisciplinary Implementation

* History
* Language arts
* Library science
* Career education
* Technology

Instructional Focus

Students will complete the Conative Character Map and will improve their abilities in:

- Making inferences
- Applying metacognition
- Accessing prior knowledge
- Using critical thinking

MAKING THE CONNECTION

Instructional Strategies and Activities

1. Ask students to work as individuals, in pairs, or in cooperative teams of three to five students.
2. Tell students to read a story, trade book, or novel about a person who achieved his or her goals through conation.
3. Challenge students to complete the Conative Character Map.

CONATIVE HOOK: Now that I *know*, what will I *do*?

Extended Research and Reflection

1. Ask students to pretend they are newspaper or television reporters who have been given the assignment to interview a family member, a teacher, a neighbor, or someone they know.
2. Have the students, in cooperative teams, develop interview questions that they will ask the interviewee regarding how he or she stayed focused and did not give up on a task, job, dream, etc.
3. Have students write or use art drawings to share the information they were able to obtain.
4. Ask students to invite their interviewee to class and share his or her experiences in person.

Help students reflect on their learning by discussing the following:

1. Did you acquire a better understanding of the character as you reflected on the traits, skills, and qualities of this person?
2. Explain your answer by giving examples from the story or incidents encountered by the character.

ASSESSMENT

Assess the success of the lesson by asking yourself the following questions:

1. Did students demonstrate interest in the reading assignment? How did they demonstrate their interest?
2. How did students demonstrate their understanding of the character and his or her actions?
3. Were students able to identify with the character personally or with someone they knew? How did they do this?
4. How effectively were students able to apply their metacognitive, literacy, and critical thinking skills? How was this evidenced?
5. Were students able to understand the underlying theme (persevering in spite of the odds)? How was this evidenced by each student?

Conative Character Map

2. How do you think the main character was able to accomplish the things he or she accomplished? Where do you think his or her strength of will and character came from?

1. List three character traits that prove the main character believed In him- or herself.

_____

_____

3. How do you think this story would have ended if the character did not have the will and determination to succeed?

____ _____

8. Name at least two people who have been influential in your life and explain why you selected these two.

_____

4. Write three things that demonstrate the main character had determination and the will to do whatever was required of him or her to achieve his or her goal.

_____

7. Explain three things that give you the incentive to never give up your attempts to be successful.

_____

5. Describe one way that you and the main character are similar.

_____

6. Give two reasons why you know you are able to succeed in whatever you put your mind to do.

_____

One, Two, Three, Just Take a Look at Me!

Character is power.—BOOKER T. WASHINGTON

WHAT'S IT ALL ABOUT?

Purpose

- To develop students' recognition of numbers and number values
- To develop students' knowledge of math concepts
- To enhance students' awareness of their talents, skills, and special gifts
- To tap into students' multiple intelligences

Instructional Objectives

- Students will use their prior knowledge.
- Students will implement math concepts.
- Students will enrich their literacy skills.
- Students will enhance their self-esteem.

Interdisciplinary Implementation

- Mathematics
- Literacy
- Character education
- Technology

Instructional Focus

Students will utilize the All About Me completion sheet to

- Consider how they perceive themselves
- Contemplate how they think others perceive them
- Think about their personal and academic abilities
- See how these qualities can help them be successful in school and life

MAKING THE CONNECTION

Instructional Strategies and Activities

1. Select a story or book to read to the students that focuses on the main character's positive qualities, heroic actions, and belief in him- or herself.

2. Ask students to identify and discuss the following:
   a. Who is the main character?
   b. What does the character do that makes him or her special?
   c. Why is the character considered a hero, a nice person, or a special friend?
   d. How does the character help others and act considerate, smart, and successful?
   e. How does the character demonstrate a belief in him- or herself?
   f. How does the character use his or her determination to achieve whatever goal he or she has set?

3. Challenge students to complete the All About Me worksheet. Explain that students can use words or pictures to express their thoughts.

CONATIVE HOOK: Now that I *know*, what will I *do*?

Extended Research and Reflections

1. Have younger students read, watch a story video, or listen to a story about animals or people who have survived difficult situations or who have demonstrated their ability to endure and not give up.

2. Have students complete a story map to demonstrate their understanding.

3. Have older students do research on a non-fictional person who has exhibited having self-assurance, determination, and belief in themselves and their abilities.

4. Have students write a paper based on their research.

Help students reflect upon the lesson by asking them the following questions:

1. Did these activities help you think about all of the character's good qualities?
2. Do you feel proud of who you are?

ASSESSMENT

Assess the success of the lesson by asking yourself the following questions:

1. Did students gain an understanding of and enhance their knowledge about the sequence of numbers? How was this knowledge demonstrated?
2. Were students able to use their prior knowledge and various cognitive and creative skills with this activity? How?
3. Were students able to demonstrate their comprehension skills? How?

All About Me

My name is_____

1 One thing I like about myself is . . .

2 Two things my family like about me are . . .

3 Three things I am really good at are . . .

4 Four things that make me the special person I am are . . .

5 Five things that help me succeed in school and outside of school are . . .

FURTHER READING

Brophy, J. (1987). Synthesis of research on strategies for motivating students to learn. *Educational Leadership, 45*(2), 40–48.

Caine, R., & Caine, G. (1994). *Making connections: Teaching and the human brain.* Menlo Park, CA: Addison-Wesley.

Cattell, R. B., & Warburton, F. W. (1967). *Objective personality and motivational tests.* Urbana: University of Illinois.

Jensen, E. (1995). *Superteaching: Success strategies that bring out the best in both you and your students.* Del Mar, CA: Turning Point.

Jensen, E. (1998). *Teaching with the brain in mind.* Alexandria, VA: Association for Supervision and Curriculum Development.

Kolbe, K. (1990). *The conative connection.* Reading, MA: Addison-Wesley.

Kostelnik, M. (1992). Myths associated with developmentally appropriate programs. *Young Children, 47*(40), 17–23.

LeDoux, J. (1996). *The emotional brain: The mysterious underpinnings of emotional life.* New York: Simon and Schuster.

Wiggins, J. S. (1979). A psychological taxonomy of trait-descriptive terms: The interpersonal domain. *Journal of Personality and Social Psychology, 37,* 395–412.

CHAPTER 5

When in Doubt...
Teach

Student

I ts difficult to allow yourself to fail—when you
know there are so many people reaching out to
help you.

—TENTH GRADE STUDENT

Teacher

I n teaching, it is impossible to hide behind a mask or label.
Working with children lends itself to introspection and
self-analysis. I know that this byproduct of teaching keeps
me coming back year after year even after I swear I'm going
to quit!

—ELEMENTARY TEACHER

Authentic Teaching in the Conative Domain

Authentic teaching is teaching at its best. Authentic teachers use the conative domain to ignite each student's desire to achieve and excel. Authentic teachers create challenging and supportive learning environments in which students engage in significant learning tasks. Teachers and learners understand that learning has intrinsic meaning; they know that learning for the sake of learning is as important as learning the required content. Authentic teachers use sound strategies that foster students' desire to learn. Because students learn to take responsibility for their own learning, teachers need not dominate and control their students, but instead they can lead and facilitate students' learning. Students are inspired to take on difficult and exciting challenges, and teachers build a learning culture that supports the growth of all students.

Authentic teaching is not complete without *caring*. Teachers must reach beyond themselves to ensure that what they teach students connects with their everyday lives. Caring is part of the teaching profession; we cannot put a price tag on it. Caring comes from knowing oneself and one's values. In *The Courage to Teach,* Palmer (1998) explains that teachers must know their "inner terrain"—they must understand themselves.

Two Small Words

To teach: These two small words represent an ongoing and tremendous task. What does it mean to teach? Sometimes it means that a child gains a hero, an educator transforms a life, the human condition is altered, the world is enlightened, a soul is touched. Sometimes it is a rare and amazing process that simply stretches beyond words.

Find Heroic Ways to Reach All Students

Must we have the will to teach? If we do, we must ask ourselves, What inspires our will to teach? What do we hope our students will learn? What have they learned from us so far? Will they learn to believe in themselves and the learning process by how we live together and how we live apart? What will they do with what they know? Hopefully, they will use everything we teach them to better themselves and the world.

"Good teaching requires self-knowledge: it is a secret hidden in plain sight" (p. 3).

Teaching in the conative domain begins when students walk into the classroom and encounter positive, caring energy. Conative teaching is teaching that cares. It is teaching that questions, seeks in-depth answers, and fosters significant learning.

Remember, students give back what they receive. If we model caring, believing, listening, understanding, and cooperating, students will imitate us. If we work together toward common goals, share ideas, model expected behavior, and mentor, students will want to learn. When we demonstrate a strong will to teach and learn, students achieve higher levels of being, knowing, and acting.

To teach means to have the courage to develop spiritual will—to foster students' inner strength and desire to learn. To teach means to have the courage to foster cultural will—to celebrate the uniqueness of every human who has lived in the past, is living in the present, and will live in the future. To teach means to have the courage to view life as opportunity—to support and transform the human condition. To teach means to have the courage to know ourselves—to invite our unknown, creative, and spiritual components to lead us into responsible action.

I Use Diverse Teaching Styles!

Current theory suggests that different teaching situations require different teaching styles (Bellanca, 1990; Bonwell and Eison, 1991; Grasha, 1996; McKeachie, 1986). Students do not learn in the same manner as they did in the era of the one-room schoolhouse. Students are no longer expected to "sit and get"—to remain quiet while the teacher imparts knowledge using the same methodology for all students. Students are much more sophisticated now than they were before the explosion of technology. Research shows that today's students pursue, perceive, and process information differently than did students a decade ago (Dunn & Dunn, 1978; Griggs, 1991; Kolb, 1984; Woods, 1994). Students have different learning styles. Therefore, teachers must use different teaching styles (including various instructional strategies, resources, and technology) to reach them.

When brought together, courage, character, and conation raise personal expectations.

The most successful teachers are able to adapt their teaching style to the unique and diverse skills and abilities of their students. A national task force sponsored by National Association of Secondary School Principals developed this definition of learning styles: "The composite of characteristic cognitive, . . . affective, and physiological factors that serve as relatively stable indicators of how a learner perceives, interacts with, and responds to the learning environment" (Keefe, 1979).

Nothing to Fear

A reporter once asked Winston Churchill to share his secret to success. He replied, "I can tell you that in just seven words: Never give up, never ever give up!" This is why we celebrate the conative spirit in learning and throughout our lives. Without it, nothing around us would exist—our homes, cars, computers, telephones, cures for diseases, travel as we know it, paper, pencils, books, ideas, research, schools, hospitals, careers, science, technology, the arts, law, psychology, literature, relationships with individuals from around the world, the information revolution, and on and on. Without conation, we would not have achieved so much, so quickly!

If teachers wish to reach students with different learning styles, they must use teaching strategies and activities that are

- differentiated;
- student-centered;
- goal-oriented;
- spirited;
- considerate;
- reflective;
- direct;
- individual and cooperative;
- inclusive;
- culturally, emotionally, and physically sensitive; and
- engaging and inviting.

I Care!

Two of the most significant contributions a teacher can make in a class-room are *caring* and *time*. Caring doesn't come wrapped in dollar bills, but the compensation for caring goes beyond what any academic test can measure. Time is something we all have while we have it. It is up to us to choose how we will use it. Those who have the will to teach all students give their students time and caring. They are sensitive to their students' needs.

Giving of yourself for a cause or an interest is an honorable way to share and invite others into your life. Teachers who have the will to teach give time and caring to reach the goal of authentic student success. Unfortunately, some teachers fail to appreciate students as individuals and are not interested in moving outside the rote domain of teaching and testing. Instead, they focus on high performance. Although high perfor-mance is a worthy goal, teachers must also instill in students a sense of meaning, fairness, belonging, hope, and empowerment to effect change. One of the best indicators that courageous teaching is taking place in a classroom is that morale is high and students are interested in learning, often even excited about learning! Teachers are paying attention to stu-dents in these classrooms. For many young people, this "paying attention" is affirming, as evidenced by the following student voices:

> Being able to ask questions and get answers or clues is helpful to me in school. In reading, I'm successful because I have a partner to read with. We help each other read smoothly and correctly. If we are unsure of what to do, our teacher guides us. Being able to have a partner motivates me to get As.
>
> —FOURTH GRADE STUDENT

> At my school, teachers take time with you and they make it seem like they really like you and care about you. Maybe it's because I listen.
>
> —FOURTH GRADE STUDENT

Acts of Courage

The conative connection transforms dreams into reality, pain into triumph, defeat into success, frustration into joy, low test scores into high test scores, low achievement into high performance, success into significance. The conative connection builds positive attitudes and productive relationships, transforms bias into open-minded objectivity, and changes negative self-fulfilling prophecies into positive acts of courage.

I Choose to Teach!

When we choose to teach, we also acknowledge that we not only choose to learn about our subject matter, but we also choose to learn about those who journey with us—students, parents, and fellow educators. We seek to understand how students see themselves and how they see the world around them (their world view). The principles of conation maintain that students can be taught that they have the power to choose to learn and to lead positive and productive lives. We must take time to help students make conative connections.

Lecturing doesn't change behavior; teaching that addresses diverse learning styles, demonstrates caring, and fosters conation changes behavior. Teachers who listen, understand, provide wisdom, and share thoughts, opinions, and facts impact students who need hope, promise, and purpose. Certainly, learning lies in the hands of the learner. We acknowledge this when we teach with conation in mind.

Testing! Testing! Testing!

Through the passion of the will, we pursue excellence. Through our pursuit of excellence, we climb—lifting others and setting them free to live, hope, and find themselves. Together we learn to run with our dreams.

Heroic Teachers

Heroic teachers know that success comes from grace, wisdom, and determination. In the process, these teachers must rebuild their shattered beliefs, roll up their sleeves, and get to work. Heroic teachers arrive at school each day—sometimes tired but always ready for whatever the day may bring.

Most students are inspired by the strength of their teachers' courage, insight, and will. Students learn quickly that these teachers can't be fooled by the masks students wear. These teachers can see behind the masks of anger, inattention, disruptive behavior, disinterest, and low test scores. They know students use these masks to hide what they don't know and are afraid to ask. They know students don't want to be ridiculed. They understand that masks are an easy way out of learning. They also know the masks hide students' true identity and cover up their conation.

Courageous teachers never stop seeking out and nurturing students' strengths. They seek to understand why certain gaps exist in students' learning and how to build bridges. They recognize teaching is not something they do *to* students, it's a journey they take *with* students. Students need responsible adults who reach out and demonstrate what it means to learn and apply new learning to life. Exemplary teachers strengthen students' assets by focusing on purposeful learning strategies that engage all students through various learning styles.

Learning from the Inside Out

We sometimes experience the negative side of human behavior in the actions of students. This misbehavior often results from the actual or perceived lack of positive nurturing and empowerment from significant others. Because the operational framework that governs the overall thinking in our culture is "He who dies with the most toys wins," one of our challenges as educators is to help students expand their thinking about life, education, and future goals. The negative social realities that exist in many of our schools are merely a reflection of the myriad of mixed messages students receive every day.

Negative Learning on Student Learning

We sometimes experience the negative side of human behavior in the actions of students. This misbehavior often results from the actual or perceived lack of positive nurturing and empowerment from significant others. Because the operational framework that governs the overall thinking in our culture is "He who dies with the most toys wins," one of our challenges as educators is to help students expand their horizons.

Three of the most common influences that negatively impact learning and student behavior are anger, apathy, and fear. Often there are variations and combinations of personal issues that block learning (see Figure 5.1).

When school means engagement we do more than take attendance.

Using STARS to Support the Will to Learn

Do you ever feel disqualified from being successful? Are you ever overtaken by a sense of uselessness or overwhelmed by feelings of inadequacy? There are times when teachers and students express insecurity.

As a teacher, sometimes you might think that you have students who really don't want to learn or have anything to do with school. Perhaps that is true for some students. So, what can you do? Use the STARS

Influences That Negatively Impact Learning

Anger/Frustration

Feeling	*Thinking*	*Acting*
Resentful	Don't tell me what to do!	Rude
Annoyed	Why do we have to do this stuff?	Stubborn
Irritated	Nobody ever listens to me.	Passive-aggressive
Disgusted	That's it! I'm not doing anything else!	Defiant
Furious	You better get away from me!	Destructive

Apathy/Boredom

Feeling	*Thinking*	*Acting*
Numb	It really doesn't matter.	Listless
Helpless	I don't know how.	Stuck
Powerless	No way, forget it.	Spaced Out
Tired	I don't know why I even come to school.	Indifferent
Depressed	It's no use.	Unresponsive

Fear/Insecurity

Feeling	*Thinking*	*Acting*
Anxious	What if I don't get it right?	Hyperactive
Confused	I don't know what to do.	Overwhelmed
Uncertain	What if I fail?	Nervous
Threatened	I wish I were someplace else.	Scared
Dread	My life depends on this test and I'm not ready.	Traumatized

Figure 5.1

The STARS of Conative Fitness

Safe and caring school climate

AND

Teacher beliefs filled with appropriate expectations

AND

Authentic and supportive accountability

LEAD TO

Resilience and high performance

AND

Stellar student-teacher relationships.

Figure 5.2

formula shown in Figure 5.2. STARS is an acronym for the factors that support and enhance conative fitness, academic energy, and high performance.

Implementing the Four I's of Teacher Leadership

Effective teachers engage all students in classroom activities by inspiring, informing, investing in, and involving students (see Figure 5.3). First, teachers inspire students to feel that they are part of something special. Students become inspired by their own desire to learn and by the teacher's commitment to the student. Second, teachers inform students through open and honest communication about goals, objectives, assignments, and expected outcomes. However, this communication should be a "two way street" in that students are allowed to communicate to, with, and back to the teacher, what they understand or do not understand, which strategies and activities are more interesting and engaging, and what "turns them on to learning." Effective teachers are willing to receive communication from students as well as convey it. Third, teachers invest in students by letting them know we want them to succeed in school and life, and that we are available to support their efforts and facilitate their learning. We demonstrate the belief that our investment in them has merit and will yield a significant return by listening to their concerns, problems, and input and by recognizing their accomplishments, accepting their failures, and appreciating their individual personalities and abilities. Fourth, teachers involve students by bringing them together to share projects, activities, and ideas. Students build peer relationships through academic and social interactions. Teachers also involve students by strengthening student-teacher relationships.

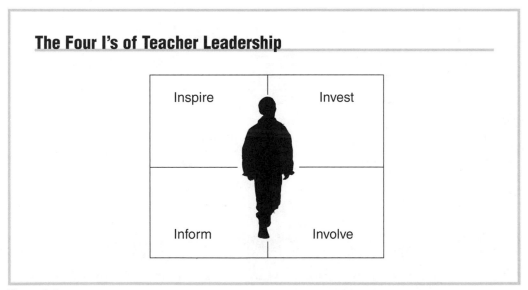

The Four I's of Teacher Leadership

Inspire

Invest

Inform

Involve

Figure 5.3

A New Day in Education

Consider this Swedish proverb: The afternoon knows what the morning never suspected. When we take time to reflect upon what we've learned throughout the day, we learn. We transform the old into new and the new into dreams for tomorrow. Healthy learning communities encourage students to be engaged and reflective in their learning, not just occupied with busywork.

Promoting Conation Schoolwide

It is not enough to promote conation in the classroom, we must also promote it throughout the school. Many schools are engaged in systemic change initiatives. Conation should be part of these initiatives.

Who Needs Assessments?

To promote conation schoolwide, we must examine how well we are meeting students' needs through our systemic change initiatives. How many needs assessments have you read (or written) regarding desired changes and outcomes for your school or organization? In many schools across the nation, there is a need for systemic change. As we seek change, we must also reflect and respond to this question: How much growth has taken place in my school in the past few years? It is critical that we take time to examine the accomplishments and recognize the practices and people who promoted the change process.

The Spirit of Conation

We can know who we are and we can realize our own power if we take time to find ourselves and acknowledge our power in the present moment. Our power is available right here, where we live and breathe, hope and dream. In the present moment, we can challenge and demand ourselves and others to be the best we can be. This is the spirit of conation.

We can examine our schools through growth assessments. A growth assessment allows us to do the following:

- Examine where we are
- Determine collectively if where we are is where we should be at this point in time
- Value our achievements (no matter how great or small)
- Ascertain whether or not our accomplishments align with our goals
- Reassess where we are going
- Evaluate how far we have come
- Build upon our strengths
- Celebrate our accomplishments
- Seek and use new team building strategies
- Explore new possibilities
- Make adjustments for continuous growth

We must regularly determine what students need to know in order to succeed in our global economy. Our school agendas must reflect the conative idea that transformational learning happens when teachers have the *will* and *determination* to teach every student with no exceptions.

Building Conation into the Curriculum

Another way to promote conation schoolwide is to include conation in the curriculum. By building a conative connection into the curriculum, teachers alter the self-repression dynamic and, instead, construct paradigms for maximal student development. When students are taught in a harmonious, mutually respectful environment, they change their behavior and increase their participation in learning. Many students want to perform well, but are often discouraged by hostile and stressful conditions at home, with peers, in school, or within themselves. The way teachers invite (or "disinvite") students to participate in classroom learning speaks volumes about what and whom they value, who they believe will or will not learn, and who deserves their support. School achievement and self-respect (viewing oneself as intellectually, emotionally, and socially capable) are not separate issues, but shared goals.

When we wonder why some students fail and others succeed, we must remember the role that students' belief systems play in achievement. We must also examine our willingness to nurture positive beliefs if we wish to promote maximal performance. When students respect themselves and we nurture that self-respect, students will be successful in their academic performance. Conation is the foundation that determines if students will choose to strive, give up, or work somewhere in between.

THE **Will** to **Teach**

Looking Back

Examine your life. Remember you have reached the place you are right now—whether good or not so good—through the actions you've taken based on your beliefs, values, life experiences, perceptions of yourself, perceptions of the world around you, and strength of will.

Reaching Past Fear and Doubt

In learning and in life, adults create the experiences, climate, and conditions in which students live and learn. If we find it difficult to imagine our own goals and dreams, then we must take time to chart new beginnings and write new chapters for ourselves. We must infuse ourselves with courage—courage to see positive outcomes in our lives and courage to realize and live out our deepest beliefs and values. Courage enables us to transcend our fears and doubts and to strive toward our personal beliefs, values, and goals.

For generations we have developed and reformed learning systems, but we've forgotten to use one of our greatest tools for effecting change—conation. We use conation in the classroom and curriculum, but forget to use it in our systemic change initiatives and in our everyday lives. If we want to be truly lifelong learners, why not strive to be the best we can be? Why not open our hearts and minds to fresh ideas, new possibilities, and the *will* to discover authentic success beyond the limitations we place on ourselves and our students?

Schools can grow students' power to succeed by promoting conation. Ideas for growing this power are shown in Figure 5.4.

Grow the Power

Schools can grow the power of personal achievement by
- modeling,
- supporting,
- guiding,
- caring,
- expecting,
- acknowledging, and
- preparing students to succeed in the best and worst conditions at school, at home, and in everyday life.

Figure 5.4

Keep Reaching and Then Just … Keep on Teaching!

Both teachers and students are driven by the *will*. A hero resides in every teacher and student. Classrooms are filled with everyday heroes. Sometimes the heroes fall asleep, because we forget to invite them into our lives (see Figure 5.5). Will we allow the hero to craft new thinking and actions in our expectations and work with students?

Think of each day as a new beginning in some child's life. You *do* make a difference. You have the power to unleash the hero from deep within your students. This hero is sometimes held hostage so that students don't recognize it within themselves. But you can help them uncover their inner hero. And once they meet their inner hero, they will never forget it.

Just Keep on Teaching!

*W*hen students come from communities
that are exploding with anger, outrage, or fear,
> **just keep on teaching.**

*W*hen students come from homes where love has been abandoned,
and dismantled by apathy, hopelessness, and despair,
> **just keep on teaching.**

*W*hen hate is just another four-letter word,
where lives are put on hold and dreams are deferred,
> **just keep on teaching.**

*W*hen students explain
that the meaning of hope is as foreign as the meaning of truth,
> **just keep on teaching**

*W*hen students' lives are fragmented,
when they don't know to whom they can turn,
when they're lost in the shadows of those who no longer dream of what can be,
step back, regroup, start reaching, and
> **just keep on teaching.**

*W*hen you work with parents whose minds are washed by television soaps,
dulled by a residue of emptiness and an inability to cope,
when ambitions are discarded by promises gone astray—
they want better for their children, but they don't know of any other way—
teach them how promises are fulfilled,
through hard work, determination, and a never-ending will.
> **Just keep on teaching**

*G*rowing up too fast, adult experiences too soon,
lives so young—but not so tender.
Where are the children?
You pause and then remember that you must
> **just keep on teaching.**

Figure 5.5

*A*lcohol-stained lives, drugs, gangs, and guns on the rise,
tension in the air and war in the streets, cries for help.
You reach some, and others you must let go,
the pain of their lifestyles weigh heavy on your soul.
Exhausted, but there you are,
a mystery of goodness, nobility of action, still giving—
     just keep on teaching.

*C*hildren wanting to belong,
thinking macho and "using" means being strong.
     Just keep on teaching.

*I*ncomprehensible is what you describe
as you look at so many of your students' lives.
If you don't reach them, who will?
     Just keep on teaching.

*B*ecoming involved in guiding their way
sometimes gets hard as you help them make it through each day.
     Just keep on teaching.

*I*nspiring students to reach up high,
because that's the place where their futures lie—
if they are to succeed, you can't give up.
     Just keep on teaching.

*E*xperiencing the feeling of doing something right,
perhaps for the first time in all of their lives.
Profound and personal, you are encouraging kids
to believe in themselves and then achieve.
     Just keep on teaching.

*Y*ou are the human voice, cultivating the winner within—
the hero some call it.
You've done it before, and you can do it again,
     just keep on teaching.

Lessons from

the **Heart**
of **Learning**

Education is not limited to a student learning how to read, write, or think critically, but it includes teaching students about interpersonal and intrapersonal relationships. Education should prepare students emotionally, psychologically, and intellectually. It is vital that students acquire core knowledge and skills, but it is also an essential part of their education to learn how to get along with and relate to others in a socially co-existence relationship.

The following lessons are designed to help students under-stand relationships and their importance. The lessons motivate students to read stories and novels focusing on a historic context, but also encourage them to examine their feelings and beliefs about themselves and their interactions with others.

Think About It!

The most important ingredient in the formula of success is knowing how to get along with people.—THEODORE ROOSEVELT

WHAT'S IT ALL ABOUT?

Purpose

* To help students become aware of their relationships with friends, family members, teachers, and others
* To develop students' awareness of and belief in their ability to solve problems
* To help students discover their own abilities to cope with challenges
* To make students aware of their abilities to succeed in life and school

Instructional Objectives

* Students will develop an understanding of the importance of relationships with others.
* Students will develop critical thinking skills through interactions with real-life situations and through literature.
* Students will enhance their knowledge and understanding of themselves.
* Students will gain an understanding of their beliefs about themselves and their gifts, skills, talents, and abilities.

Interdisciplinary Implementation

* Conflict resolution
* Language arts
* Reading
* Career education
* Technology

Instructional Focus

Students will complete the Semantic Feature Analysis and will improve their abilities in

* making inferences,
* accessing prior knowledge,
* applying metacognition, and
* using critical thinking.

MAKING THE CONNECTION

Instructional Strategies and Activities

1. As a class, read "The Little Red Hen" or a similar story that features the theme of relationships between people or animals.
2. Encourage students to compare the Little Red Hen's attitude and behavior to the attitudes and behaviors of the other animals.
   a. Draw a Semantic Feature Analysis chart (as shown on the next page) to help students determine specific traits about the various animals.
   b. Discuss each animal's attitudes and behaviors. Ask students to designate the traits each animal exhibited by placing a mark in the appropriate boxes on the chart.
3. Ask students: Why do you think the duck (cat, dog) was unhelpful (uncooperative, inconsiderate, etc.)?
4. Challenge students to examine their own attitudes and behaviors:
   a. Are there times when you are unhelpful (uncaring, uncooperative, etc.)?
   b. What can you do to correct your actions?
5. Encourage students to name the good character traits that the Little Red Hen possessed.

CONATIVE HOOK: Now that I *know*, what will I *do*?

Extended Research and Reflection

Challenge students to retell this story by drawing their own pictures of what happened. Explain that the pictures should be placed in sequence according to the events that took place in the story.

Encourage students to reflect on their learning by answering the following questions:

1. What did you learn from the story?
2. Why do you think that the Little Red Hen did not become discouraged when none of the other animals would help?
3. Was it fair of the Little Red Hen to refuse to share the bread with the other animals? Explain your answer.

Semantic Feature Analysis

Animals	Helpful	Unhelpful	Cooperative	Uncooperative	Caring	Uncaring	Considerate
Duck							
Cat							
Dog							
Little Red Hen							

ASSESSMENT

Assess the success of the lesson by asking yourself the following questions:
1. Did students participate in the oral discussions?
2. Were students able to retell the story correctly in their drawings?
3. Did students exhibit an understanding of the significance of the story?
4. Were students able to relate and reflect on their own behaviors and traits?

What If…?

History, despite its wrenching pain, cannot be unlived, but if faced with courage, need not be lived again.—MAYA ANGELOU

WHAT'S IT ALL ABOUT?

Purpose

- To promote students' interest in historical events and people
- To help students, through authentic tasks, understand how the past can affect the present
- To encourage students to use their creative and critical thinking skills

Instructional Objectives

- Students will develop a knowledge base about historical events and people.
- Students will become more interested in history.
- Students will connect historical events to current events.

Interdisciplinary Implementation

- History
- Language arts
- Career development
- Character education

Instructional Focus

Students will read the special report on the Civil War and reflect on the following issues:

- how the outcomes of historical events have impacted on current events
- how history can teach us how to prepare for a better future
- why learning and knowing about history can be interesting and informative

MAKING THE CONNECTION

Instructional Strategies and Activities

1. Explain to students that an important project has been assigned to station INFORM-TV. The station is accepting applications for these positions:
   - Reporter
   - News writer
   - Editor
   - Television producer
   - Researcher
   - Graphic artist
   - Television news anchor

   List the positions on the board and ask each student to select the job(s) for which they wish to apply. Explain that more than one person can work at each job.

2. Challenge students to apply for the jobs by writing a letter to the executive producer that explains why they would like a certain position, their qualifications, and why they would be the best person for the position. Ask the class to determine how applicants will be selected.

3. Explain that this project involves "reconstructing" history. Tell students to choose a particular event in history from the Historical Events list (on the next page). You can also encourage students to think of other events they might like to study.

4. If students do not know the details about this event, encourage them to do some research. (Remember, a primary purpose of this lesson is to challenge students to broaden their knowledge base about historical events.) Discuss what led up to the event, what incidents occurred, and the outcome.

5. Challenge students to explain what they think the country, the world, or the fate of certain racial or religious groups might be today if things had turned out differently. (For an example, see the Special Report on page 147.)

6. Place students in teams. Try to have as many of the roles (editor, graphic artist, etc.) represented in each group as possible.

HISTORICAL EVENTS

American colonies win independence from England

North defeats the South in the Civil War

Japan bombs Pearl Harbor

Great Depression of 1929

Mass production of the automobile

Mexican revolution

Dropping of the atomic bomb at Hiroshima

Industrial Revolution

Bay of Pigs

Harlem Renaissance

Interment of Japanese-Americans

The Holocaust

SPECIAL REPORT

The South has won the Civil War! Confederate soldiers were victorious over the ill-prepared Union Army. The surviving Northern troops are preparing to gather their wounded and dead and return to their homes in the North. As a result of this astounding victory, there will be no changes in the current policy regarding the owning of slaves.

Now the South can return to its regal way of life. We can start to rebuild our plantations, get our crops planted, and continue the way of life that our ancestors left us as a rightful legacy and that we can now leave to our children and our children's children.

We will continue to take care of our slaves as we have always done. We will ensure that they are fed, clothed, and cared for as long as they remain our property and on our plantations. They are happy with their way of life and did not welcome the changes that President Lincoln tried to force on them. We are happy that the South will be able to resume our beautiful way of life. Long live the South!

7. Challenge teams to gather information about the event and then rewrite and reconstruct the event. In other words, students will take a quantum leap or travel on a time machine back to the event and change the face of history. Encourage teams to make graphics to illustrate their stories.

8. When teams are finished, ask the news anchors to present the team reports.

CONATIVE HOOK: Now that I *know*, what will I *do*?

Extended Research and Reflection

1. Ask students to reread this quote by Maya Angelou: "History, despite its wrenching pain, cannot be unlived, but if faced with courage, need not be lived again." Challenge students to research Maya Angelou's life and answer the following questions:

   a. What is her profession, career, or vocation?

   b. What are her beliefs, values, and views about life, the world, and people?

   c. What are some other books, poems, and statements made by Maya Angelou that provide insight into her character, convictions, and viewpoints?

   d. How does her writing reflect her beliefs and values?

2. Use the graphic organizer on the next page to depict the causes and effects of a historical event that the class is currently studying or has studied in the past.

Ask students to think about some positive deed they did that resulted in making someone happy, or caused some changes either in their lives or someone else's life.

Ask students to think about a famous person in history they may have read about and reflect on the following questions:

1. What character traits did this person possess?

2. Do you think his or her traits contributed to this person's accomplishments or actions? Explain how.

3. Did this person have traits that you would like to have, or that you possibly already possess? Explain your answer.

CAUSE & EFFECT GRAPHIC ORGANIZER

Cause	*Effect*
The events that happened were:	*As a result, this is what happened:*

Write a summary, listing the primary causes or events that took place, leading to or resulting in the _____.

List and explain the effects these events had on _____'s history then and now.

4. Do you think your famous person in history could have achieved what he or she did without the character traits you named? Explain your answer.

ASSESSMENT

Assess the success of the lesson by asking yourself the following questions:

1. How did students use their writing skills?
2. How did students demonstrate their decision-making skills?
3. How well were teams able to work together?
4. Did students increase their knowledge about historical events, people, and places? How was this knowledge demonstrated?

FURTHER READING

Armstrong, T. (1998). *Awakening genius in the classroom*. Alexandria, VA: Association for Supervision and Curriculum Development.

Barr, R., & Parrett, W. (2003). *Saving our students, saving our schools: 50 proven strategies for revitalizing at-risk students and low-performing schools.* Glenview, IL: Pearson Professional Development.

Danielson, C. (1996). *Enhancing professional practice: A framework for teaching.* Alexandria, VA: Association for Supervision and Curriculum Development.

Marzano, R. J. (2003). *What works in schools: Transforming research into action.* Alexandria, VA: Association for Supervision and Curriculum Development.

Bibliography

Allee, V. (1997). *The knowledge evolution.* Newton, MA: Butterworth-Heinemann.

Allers, R., & Minkoff, R. (Directors). (1994). *The Lion King.* United States: Walt Disney Pictures.

Allington, R. L., & Cunningham, P. M. (2002). *Schools that work: Where all children read and write* (2nd ed.). Boston: Allyn and Bacon.

Alpert, R., & Haber, R. (1960). Anxiety in academic achievement situations. *Journal of Abnormal and Social Psychology, 61,* 207–215.

American Heritage® Dictionary of the English Language (4th ed.). (2000). Conation. Boston: Houghton Mifflin.

Ames, C. (1992). Classrooms: Goals, structures, and student motivation. *Journal of Educational Psychology, 84,* 261–271.

Ames, C., & Ames, R. (1984). Systems of student and teacher motivation: Toward a qualitative definion. *Journal of Educational Psychology, 76,* 535.

Ames, C., & Archer, J. (1988). Achievement goals in the classroom: Students' learning strategies and motivation processes. *Journal of Educational Psychology, 80,* 260–267.

Amrein, A. L., & Berliner, D. C. (2003). The effects of high-stakes testing on student motivation and learning. *Educational Leadership, 60*(5), 32–37.

Anderman, E. M., & Midgley, C. (1996, March). *Changes in achievement goal orientations after the transition to middle school.* Paper presented at the Biennial Meeting of the Society for Research on Adolescence, Boston, MA. (ERIC Document Reproduction Service No. ED396226)

Anderson, C. (1983). Motivational and performance deficits in interpersonal settings: The effects of attributional style. *Journal of Personality and Social Psychology, 45,* 1136–1147.

Annarella, L. (2001). Goal setting: An important part of teaching. *Educational Horizons Archives.* Retrieved October 7, 2003 from http://www.pilambda.org/horizons/v79-2/annarella.pdf.

Argyris, C., & Schon, D. (1978). *Organizational learning.* Reading, MA: Addison-Wesley.

Armstrong, T. (1994). *Multiple intelligences in the classroom.* Alexandria, VA: Association for Supervision and Curriculum Development.

Armstrong, T. (1998). *Awakening genius in the classroom.* Alexandria, VA: Association for Supervision and Curriculum Development.

Arnold, K. D. (1995). *Lives of promise: What becomes of high school valedictorians: A fourteen-year study of achievement and life choices.* San Francisco: Jossey-Bass.

Assagioli, R. (1973). *The act of the will.* New York: Viking.

Atkinson, J. W., & Birch, D. (1978). *An introduction to motivation* (Rev. ed.). New York: Van Nostrand.

Atkinson, J. W., & Feather, N. T. (1966). *A theory of achievement motivation.* New York: Wiley.

Atkinson, J. W., & McClelland, D. C. (1948). The projective expression of needs: The effect of different intensities of the hunger drive on thematic apperception. *Journal of Experimental Psychology, 38,* 643–658.

Bagley, C., & Hunter, B. (1992). Constructivism and technology: Forging a new relationship. *Educational Technology, 32*(7), 22–27.

Bagozzi, R. (1992). The self-regulation of attitudes, intentions, and behavior. *Social Psychology Quarterly, 55*(2), 178–204.

Bain, H. P., & Jacobs, R. (1990). The case for smaller classes and better teachers. *Streamlined Seminar, 9*(1). (ERIC Document Reproduction Service No. ED322632)

Balkcom, S. (1992). *Cooperative learning: What is it?* Washington, DC: Office of Educational Research and Improvement. (ERIC Document Reproduction Service No. ED346999)

Bandura, A. (1977). Self-efficacy: Toward a unifying theory of behavioral change. *Psychological Review, 84*(2), 191–215.

Bandura, A. (1986). *Social foundations of thought and action: A social-cognitive theory.* Upper Saddle River, NJ: Prentice-Hall.

Bandura, A. (1997). *Self-efficacy: The exercise of control.* New York: W. H. Freeman.

Banks, J. A. (1988). Ethnicity, class, cognitive, and motivational styles: Research and teaching implications. *Journal of Negro Education, 57*(4), 452–466.

Barell, J. (1995). *Critical issue: Working toward student self-direction and personal efficacy as educational goals.* Oak Brook, IL: North Central Regional Educational Laboratory. Retrieved October 7, 2003 from http://www.ncrel.org/ncrel/sdrs/areas/issues/students/learning/lr200.htm.

Barr, R., & Parrett, W. (2003). *Saving our students, Saving our schools: 50 proven strategies for revitalizing at-risk students and low-performing schools.* Glenview, IL: Pearson Professional Development.

Barrett, B. (1931). *Strength of will and how to develop it.* New York: Ruland B. Smith.

Baumeister, R., Bratslavsky, E., Muraven, M., & Tice, D. (1998). Ego depletion: Is the active self a limited resource? *Journal of Personality and Social Psychology, 74*(5), 1252–1265.

Beamon, G. (2001). *Teaching with adolescent learning in mind.* Arlington Heights, IL: SkyLight Professional Development.

Beatty, M., Forst, C., & Stewart, R. (1986). Communication apprehension and motivation as predictors of public speaking duration. *Communication Education, 35*(2), 143–146.

Beck, A. (1976). *Cognitive theory and emotional disorders.* New York: International Universities Press.

Bellanca, J. (1990). *The cooperative think tank: Graphic organizers to teach thinking in the cooperative classroom.* Palatine, IL: IRI/SkyLight Training and Publishing.

Berendt, P. R., & Koski, B. (1999). No shortcuts to success. *Educational Leadership, 56*(6), 45–47.

Blachowicz, C., & Ogle, D. (2001). *Reading comprehension: Strategies for independent learners.* New York: Guilford Press.

Bloom, B. S., Engelhart, M. D., Furst, E. J., Hill, W. H., & Kratwohl, D. R. (1956). *Taxonomy of educational objectives: The classification of educational goals, By a committee of college and university examiners.* New York: Longmans, Green.

Blumenfeld, P. C. (1992). Classroom learning and motivation: Clarifying and expanding goal theory. *Journal of Educational Psychology, 84*(3), 272–281.

Blustein, D. L., Prezioso, M. S., & Schultheiss, D. P. (1995). Attachment theory and career development: Current status and future directions. *The Counseling Psychologist, 23*(3), 416–432.

Boethel, M. (1996). *The promise and challenges of constructivist professional development: A review of the literature of the SCIMAST approach.* Unpublished manuscript, Southwest Educational Development Laboratory.

Boethel, M., & Dimock, V. (1999). *Constructing knowledge with technology: A review of the literature.* Austin, TX: Southwest Educational Development Laboratory.

Bohlin, K. E. (Ed.). (2000). Can virtue be taught in the university? *Journal of Education, 182*(2).

Bonwell, C. C., & Eison, J. A. (1991). *Active learning: Creating excitement in the classroom.* (ASHE-ERIC Higher Education Report No. 1). Washington, DC: George Washington University.

Borich, G. D. (2000). *Effective teaching methods* (4th ed.). Upper Saddle River, NJ: Merrill.

Borkowski, J. G., Estrada, M. T., Milstead, M., & Hale, C. A. (1989). General problem-solving skills: Relations between metacognition and strategic processing. *Learning Disability Quarterly, 12*(1), 57-70.

Bransford, J. D., Brown, A. L., & Cocking, R. R. (1999). *How people learn: Brain, mind, experience, and school* (Committee on Developments in the Science of Learning, Commission on Behavioral and Social Sciences and Education, National Research Council). Washington, DC: National Academy Press.

Bridges, W. (1994). *JobShift: How to prosper in a workplace without jobs.* Reading, MA: Addison-Wesley.

Brooks, J. G., & Brooks, M. G. (1993). *In search of understanding: The case for constructivist classrooms.* Alexandria, VA: Association for Supervision and Curriculum Development.

Brophy, J. (1987). Synthesis of research on strategies for motivating students to learn. *Educational Leadership, 45*(2), 40–48.

Brown, D. A. (1970). *Bury my heart at Wounded Knee: An Indian history of the American West.* New York: Holt, Rinehart & Winston.

Bruner, J. (1996). *The culture of education.* Cambridge, MA: Harvard University.

Brunstein, J., & Gollwitzer, P. (1996). Effects of failure on subsequent performance: The importance of self-defining goals. *Journal of Personality and Social Psychology, 70,* 395–407.

Buck, R. (1999). The biology of affects: A typology. *Psychological Review, 106,* 301–336.

Bulter, G., & Hope, T. (1995). *Managing your mind: The mental fitness guide.* New York: Oxford University.

Buscaglia, L. (1983). *Living, loving, and learning.* New York: Fawcett Columbine.

Cacioppo, J. T., & Petty, R. E. (1982). The need for cognition. *Journal of Personality and Social Psychology, 42,* 116–131.

Caine, R., & Caine, G. (1994). *Making connections: Teaching and the human brain.* Menlo Park, CA: Addison-Wesley.

Campbell, L., & Campbell, B. (1999). *Multiple intelligences and student achievement.* Alexandria, VA: Association for Supervision and Curriculum Development.

Canfield, J., & Wells, H. C. (1994). *100 ways to enhance self-concept in the classroom: A handbook for teachers, counselors, and group leaders* (2nd ed.). Boston: Prentice Hall.

Cassidy, T., & Lynn, R. (1989). A multifactorial approach to achievement motivation: The development of a comprehensive measure. *Journal of Occupational Psychology, 62,* 301–312.

Cawelti, G. (Ed.). (1999). *Handbook of research on improving student achievement* (2nd ed.). Arlington, VA: Educational Research Service.

Clark, D. L., & Astuto, T. A. (1994). Redirecting reform: Challenges to popular assumptions about teachers and students. *Phi Delta Kappan, 75*(7), 512–520.

Classroom Connect. (1997). *Internet curriculum planning system.* Lancaster, PA: Author.

Cliff, N. (1977). Further study of cognitive processing models for inventory response. *Applied Psychological Measurement, 1,* 41–49.

Cohen, D. K., McLaughlin, M. L. W., & Talbert, J. F. (1993). *Teaching for understanding: Challenges for policy and practice.* San Francisco: Jossey-Bass.

Coles, R. (1997). *The moral intelligence of children.* New York: Random.

Collins, D. (1997). *Achieving your vision of professional development: How to assess your needs and get what you want.* Greensboro, NC: SouthEastern Regional Vision for Education (SERVE).

Cooke, G. (2002). *Keys to success for urban school principals.* Arlington Heights, IL: SkyLight Professional Development.

Corno, L. (1986). The metacognitive control components of self-regulated learning. *Contemporary Educational Psychology, 11*(4), 333–346.

Corno, L. (1989). Self-regulated learning: A volitional analysis. In B. J. Zimmerman & D. H. Schunk (Eds.), *Self-regulated learning and academic achievement: Theory, research, and practice* (pp. 111–142). New York: Springer-Verlag.

Corno, L. (1992). Encouraging students to take responsibility for learning and performance. *Elementary School Journal, 93*(1), 69–83.

Corno, L., & Kanfer, R. (1993). The role of volition in learning and performance. *Review of Research in Education, 19,* 301–341.

Covey, S. (1990). *Seven habits of highly effective people.* New York: Simon and Schuster.

Crandall, V. C., Katkovsky, W., & Crandall, V. J. (1965). Childrens' beliefs in their own control of reinforcement in intellectual–academic situations. *Child Development, 36,* 91–109.

Crawford, P. A. (1995). Early literacy: Emerging perspectives. *Journal of Research in Childhood Education, 10*(1), 71–84.

Cronbach, L. J. (1990). *Essentials of psychological testing.* New York: Harper and Row.

Csikszentmihalyi, M. (1990). *Flow: The psychology of optimal experience.* New York: Harper and Row.

Curry, L. (1990). *Learning styles in secondary schools: A review of instruments and implications for their use.* Madison: University of Wisconsin, Center for Effective Secondary Schools.

Damon, W. (1999, August). The moral development of children. *Scientific American, 281,* 72–78.

Damon, W. (Ed.). (2002). *Bringing in a new era in character education.* Stanford, CA: Hoover Institution.

Danielson, C. (1996). *Enhancing professional practice: A framework for teaching.* Alexandria, VA: Association for Supervision and Curriculum Development.

Danielson, C. (2002). *Enhancing student achievement: A framework for school improvement.* Alexandria, VA: Association for Supervision and Curriculum Development.

de Boeck, P. (1978). Validity of a cognitive processing model for responses to adjective and sentence type inventories. *Applied Psychological Measurement, 5,* 481–492.

Deci, E. L., & Ryan, R. M. (1985). *Intrinsic motivation and self determination in human behavior.* New York: Plenum.

Deiro, J. (1996). *Teaching with heart: Making healthy connections with students.* Thousand Oaks, CA: Corwin Press.

Dennett, D. C. (1978). Skinner skinned. In D. C. Dennett, *Brainstorms: Philosophical essays on mind and psychology* (pp. 53–70). Cambridge, MA: Bradford.

Dewey, J. (1933). *How we think.* Boston: D. C. Heath.

Diener, C. I., & Dweck, C. S. (1978). An analysis of learned helplessness: Continuous changes in performance, strategy, and achievement cognitions following failure. *Journal of Personality and Social Psychology, 36*(5), 451–462.

Diener, C. I., & Dweck, C. S. (1980). An analysis of learned helplessness II: The processing of success. *Journal of Personality and Social Psychology, 47,* 580–592.

Dole, J. A., Duffy, G. G., Roehler, L. R., & Pearson, P. D. (1991). Moving from the old to the new: Research on reading comprehension instruction. *Review of Educational Research, 61*(2), 239–264.

Domino, G. (1968). Differential predictions of academic achievement in conforming and independent settings. *Journal of Educational Psychology, 59,* 256–260.

Domino, G. (1971). Interactive effects of achievement orientation and teaching style on academic achievement. *Journal of Educational Psychology, 62,* 427–431.

Donagan, A. (1987). *Choice, The essential element in human action.* London: Routledge Kegan Paul.

Dretske, F. (1981). *Knowledge and the flow of information.* Cambridge, MA: Massachusetts Institute of Technology.

Druva, C., & Anderson, R. D. (1983). Science teacher characteristics by teacher behavior and by student outcome: A meta-analysis of research. *Journal of Research in Science Teaching, 20*(5), 467–479.

Dunn, R., & Dunn, K. (1978). *Teaching students through their individual learning styles: A practical approach.* Reston, VA: Reston Publishing.

Dweck, C. S. (1975). The role of expectations and attributions in the alleviation education. *Journal of Educational Psychology, 77,* 683–692.

Dweck, C. S. (1986). Motivational processes affecting learning. *American Psychologist, 41*(10), 1040–1048.

Dweck, C. S., & Leggett, E. L. (1988). A social-cognitive approach to motivation and personality. *Psychological Review 95*(2), 256–273.

Edmonds, R. (1979). Effective schools for the urban poor. *Educational Leadership, 37*(1), 15–18, 20–24.

Edwards, P., Pleasants, H. M., & Franklin, S. H. (1999). *A path to follow: Listen to parents.* Portsmouth, NH: Heinemann.

Eisner, E. W. (1991). What really counts in schools. *Educational Leadership, 48*(5), 10–11, 14–17.

Eisner, E. W. (1992a). The federal reform of schools: Looking for the silver bullet. *Phi Delta Kappan, 73*(9), 722–723.

Eisner, E. W. (1992b). The misunderstood role of the arts in human development. *Phi Delta Kappan, 73*(8), 591–595.

Elias, M. J., Zins, J. E., Weissberg, R. P., Frey, K. S., Greenberg, M. T., Haynes, N. M., Kessler, R., Schwab-Stone, M. E., & Shriver, T. P. (1997). *Promoting social and emotional learning: Guidelines for educators.* Alexandria, VA: Association for Supervision and Curriculum Develoment.

Elliott, P. (1986). Right (or left) brain cognition, wrong metaphor for creative behavior: It is prefrontal lobe volition that makes the difference in the release of creative potential. *Journal of Creative Behavior, 20*(3), 202–214.

Elliott, E. S., & Dweck, C. S. (1988). Goals: An approach to motivation and achievement. *Journal of Personality and Social Psychology, 54,* 5–12.

Ellis, A. K., & Fouts, J. T. (1997). *Research on educational innovations.* Larchmont, NY: Eye on Education.

Ellsworth, J. H. (1994). *Education on the Internet.* Indianapolis: Sams.

Ely, D. P., et al. (1996). *Trends in educational technology 1995.* Syracuse, NY: Information Resources Publications, Syracuse University. (ERIC Document Reproduction Service No. ED396717)

Emmons, R. (1986). Personal strivings: An approach to personality and subjective well-being. *Journal of Personality and Social Psychology, 51,* 1058–1068.

English, H., & English, A. (1958). *A comprehensive dictionary of psychological and psychoanalytical terms.* New York: Longmans, Green.

Entwistle, N. (1987a). A model of the teaching-learning process derived from research on student learning. In J. T. E. Richardson, M. W. Eysenck, & D. Warren Piper (Eds.), *Student learning: Research in education and cognitive psychology* (pp. 13–28). Philadelphia: Open University Press.

Entwistle, N. (1987b). *Understanding classroom learning.* London: Hodder and Stoughton.

Entwistle, N., & Ramsden, P. (1983). *Understanding student learning.* London: Groom Helm.

Epstein, J. L. (1995). School/family/community partnerships: Caring for the children we share. *Phi Delta Kappan, 76*(9), 701–712.

Epstein, J. L. (2001). *School, family, and community partnerships: Preparing educators and improving schools.* Boulder, CO: Westview.

Epstein, S. (1990). Cognitive-experiential self-theory. In L. A. Pervin (Ed.), *Handbook of personality: Theory and research* (pp. 165–191). New York: Guilford.

Erickson, E. (1968). *Identity: Youth in crisis.* New York: W. W. Norton.

Eysenck, H. J., & Eysenck, M. W. (1985). *Personality and individual differences.* New York: Plenum.

Fennimore, T. F., & Tinzmann, M. B. (1990). *What is a thinking curriculum?* Oak Brook, IL: North Central Regional Educational Laboratory. Retrieved October 7, 2003 from http://www.ncrel.org/sdrs/areas/rpl_esys/thinking.htm.

Festinger, L. (1957). *A theory of cognitive dissonance.* Evanston, IL: Row, Peterson.

Fetler, M. (1999). High school staff characteristics and mathematics test results. *Educational Policy Analysis Archives, 7*(9). (ERIC Document Reproduction Service No. EJ588920)

Fineman, S. (1977). The achievement motive construct and its measurement: Where are we now? *British Journal of Psychology, 68*, 1–22.

Ford, E., & Ford, D. H. (1987). *Humans as self-constructing living systems.* Hillsdale, NJ: Lawrence Erlbaum.

Fosnot, C. (1992). Constructing constructivism. In T. Duffy & D. Jonassen (Eds.), *Constructivism and the technology of instruction, A conversation* (pp. 167–176). Hillsdale, NJ: Lawrence Erlbaum.

Foucault, M. (1988). Technologies of the self. In L. Martin, H. Gutman, & P. Hutton (Eds.), *Technologies of the self* (pp. 16–49). Amherst: University of Massachusetts.

Fowler, C. (1989). The arts are essential to education. *Educational Leadership, 47*(3), 60–63.

Frank, A. (1956). *Anne Frank: The diary of a young girl.* (Translated by B. M. Moojart-Doubleday). New York: Random House.

Frankfurt, H. (1982). Freedom of the will and the concept of a person. In G. Watson (Ed.), *Free will* (pp. 96–110). Oxford: Oxford University.

Frankl, V. (1998). *Man's search for meaning* (Rev. ed.). New York: Washington Square.

Freeman, R. (1991). *The Wright brothers: How they invented the airplane.* New York: Holiday House.

Fried, R. L. (2001). *The passionate learner . . . How teachers and parents can help children reclaim the joy of discovery.* Boston: Beacon Press.

Frymier, A. B., & Shulman, G. (1995). What's in it for me?: Increasing content relevance to enhance students' motivation. *Communication Education, 44*(1), 40–50.

Fullan, M. (1993). *Change forces.* New York: Falmer.

Gaines, S. O., Jr., Panter, A. T., Lyde, M. D., Steers, W. N., Rusbult, C. E., Cox, C. L., & Wexler, M. O. (1997). Evaluating the circumplexity of interpersonal traits and the manifestation of interpersonal traits in interpersonal trust. *Journal of Personality and Social Psychology, 73,* 610–623.

Gardner, H. (1989). Beyond a modular view of mind. In W. Damon (Ed.), *Child development today and tomorrow* (pp. 222–239). San Francisco: Jossey-Bass.

Gardner, H. (1993). *Frames of mind: The theory of multiple intelligences* (10th anniversary ed.). New York: Basic Books.

Garmezy, N. (1991). Resiliency and vulnerability to adverse developmental outcomes associated with poverty. *American Behavioral Scientist, 34*(4), 416–430.

Gelzheiser, L., & d'Angelo, C. (2000). Historical fiction and informational texts that support social studies standards: An annotated bibliography. *The Language and Literacy Spectrum, 10,* 26–39.

Gersick, C., & Hackman, J. (1990). Habitual routines in task-performing groups. *Organizational Behavior and Human Decision Processes, 47,* 65–97.

Gholar, C., Givens, S., McPherson, M., & Riggs, E. (1991, April). *Wellness begins when the child comes first: The relationship between the conative domain and the school achievement paradigm.* Paper presented at the annual convention of the American Association for Counseling and Development, Reno, NV.

Giroux, H. A. (1988). *Teachers as intellectuals: Toward a critical pedagogy of learning.* Granby, MA: Bergin and Garvey.

Godfrey, R. (1992). Civilization, education, and the visual arts: A personal manifesto. *Phi Delta Kappan, 73*(8), 596–598, 600.

Goldschmidt, P., & Wang, J. (1999). When can schools affect dropout behavior? A longitudinal multilevel analysis. *American Educational Research Journal, 36*(4), 715–738.

Goleman, D. (1995). *Emotional intelligence: Why it can matter more than IQ for char-acter, health and lifelong achievement.* New York: Bantam.

Gollwitzer, P. (1996). Action phases and mind-sets. In E. Higgins & R. Sorrentino (Eds.), *Handbook of motivation and cognition, Vol. 2* (pp. 53–92). New York: Guilford.

Goodlad, J. L. (1984). *A place called school: Prospects for the future.* New York: McGraw-Hill.

Goodlad, J. L. (1994). *Educational renewal: Better teachers, better schools.* San Francisco: Jossey-Bass.

Goodnow, J. J. (1980). Everyday concepts of intelligence and its development. In N. Warren (Ed.), *Studies in cross-cultural psychology, Vol. 2* (pp. 191–219). Oxford: Pergamon.

Gottfried, J., & McFeely, M. G. (1997). Learning all over the place: Integrating laptop computers into the classroom. *Learning and Leading with Technology, 25* (4), 6–11.

Grasha, A. F. (1996). *Teaching with style: A practical guide to enhancing learning by understanding teaching and learning styles.* Pittsburgh, PA: Alliance.

Griggs, S. A. (1991). *Learning styles counseling.* Ann Arbor, MI: University of Michigan, ERIC Counseling and Personnel Services.

Gunning, T. (2000). *Creating literacy instruction for all children.* Boston: Allyn and Bacon.

Guthrie, J. T., Wigfield, A., & VonSecker, C. (2000). Effects of integrated instruc-tion on motivation and strategy use in reading. *Journal of Educational Psychology, 92*(2), 331–341.

Haines, J. (1996). *Stories without endings: Ash-Shadid— "The Witness."* Upper Saddle River, NJ: Globe Fearon.

Hale-Benson, J. E. (1986). *Black children: Their roots, culture, and learning styles* (Rev. ed.). Baltimore, MD: Johns Hopkins University.

Hargreaves, A. (1994). *Changing teachers, changing times.* New York: Teachers College Press.

Harlan, J. C., & Rowland, S. T. (2002). *Behavior management strategies for teachers: Achieving instructional effectiveness, student success, and student motivation—Every teacher and any student can!* (2nd ed.). Springfield, IL: Charles C. Thomas.

Harmin, M. (1995). *Strategies to inspire active learning.* Edwardsville, IL: Inspiring Strategy Institute.

Harris, J. (1994). Opportunities in work clothes: On-line problem-solving proj-ect structures. *The Computing Teacher, 21*(7), 52–55.

Harter, S. (1981). A new self-report scale of intrinsic vs. extrinsic orientation in the classroom: Motivational and informational components. *Developmental Psychology, 17*, 300–312.

Harter, S., & Connell, J. P. (1984). A model of children's achievement and related self-perceptions of competence, control, and motivational orientation. *Advances in Motivation and Achievement, 3,* 219–250.

Haycock, K. (1998). *Good teaching matters.* Washington, DC: Education Trust.

Healy, J. (1994). *Your child's growing mind: A guide to learning and brain development from birth to adolescence* (New ed.). New York: Doubleday.

Healy, J. (1999). *Endangered minds: Why children don't think—And what we can do about it.* New York: Simon and Schuster.

Heckhausen, H. (1967). *The anatomy of achievement motivation.* New York: Academic.

Heckhausen, H. (1977). Achievement motivation and its constructs: A cognitive model. *Motivation and Emotion, 1,* 283–329.

Heckhausen, H., & Kuhl, J. (1985). From wishes to action: The dead ends and shortcuts on the long way to action. In M. Frese & J. Sarini (Eds.), *Goal-directed behavior: Psychological theory and research on action* (pp. 134–159). Hillsdale, NJ: Lawrence Erlbaum.

Heckhausen, H., Schmalt, H. D., & Schneider, K. (1985). *Achievement motivation in perspective.* Orlando, FL: Academic.

Heckhausen, J., & Dweck, C. (Eds.). (1998). *Motivation and self-regulation across the life span.* New York: Cambridge University Press.

Hembree, R. (1988). Correlates, causes, effects, and treatment of test anxiety. *Review of Educational Research, 58*(1), 47–77.

Herman, J. (1990). Action plans to make your vision a reality. *NASSP Bulletin, 74*(523), 14–17.

Hershberger, W. (1987). Of course there can be an empirical science of volitional action. *American Psychologist, 42,* 1032–1033.

Hershberger, W. (1988). Psychology as a conative science. *American Psychologist, 43*(10), 823–824.

Hershberger, W. (Ed.). (1989). *Volitional action: Conation and control.* Amsterdam: Elsevier Science.

Higgins, E. T. (1987). Self-discrepancy: A theory relating self and affect. *Psychological Review, 94,* 319–340.

Hilgard, E. R. (1980). The trilogy of mind: Cognition, affection, and conation. *Journal of the History of Behavioral Sciences, 16,* 107–117.

Hilliard, Asa, III. (1991). Do we have the will to educate all children? *Educational Leadership, 49*(1), 31–36.

Hixson, J., Gholar, C., & Riggs, E. (1999). *Ensuring success for "low yield" students: Building lives and molding futures.* Retrieved October 7, 2003 from http://www.tcachstream.com.

Ho, D. (1995). Internalized culture, culturocentrism, and transcendance. *Counseling Psychologist, 23*(1), 4–24.

Hoerr, T. R. (1996). Collegiality: A new way to define instructional leadership. *Phi Delta Kappan, 77*(5), 380–381.

Hom, H. L., Jr., & Murphy, M. D. (1983). Low achiever's performance: The positive impact of a self-directed goal. *Personality and Social Psychology Bulletin, 11,* 275–285.

Horowitz, L. M., Krasnoperova, E. N., Tatar, D. G., Hansen, M. B., Person, E. A., Galvin, K. L., & Nelson, K. L. (2001). The way to console may depend on the goal: Experimental studies of social support. *Journal of Experimental Social Psychology, 37,* 49–61.

Howe, M. J. A., Davidson, J. W., & Sloboda, J. A. (1998). Innate talents: Reality or myth? *Behavioral and Brain Sciences, 21,* 399–442.

Huitt, W. (1995/1999). *Success in the information age: A paradigm shift.* Valdosta, GA: Valdosta State University. Retrieved October 7, 2003 from http://chiron.valdosta.edu/whuitt/col/context/infoage.html.

Huitt, W. (1999). *Conation as an important factor of mind.* Retrieved October 7, 2003 from http://chiron.valdosta.edu/whuitt/col/regsys/conation.html.

Hunsley, J. (1987). Cognitive processes in mathematics anxiety and test anxiety: The role of appraisals, internal dialogue, and attributions. *Journal of Educational Psychology, 79,* 388–392.

Hutchinson encyclopedia. (2000). Conation. Oxford: Helicon.

Hyerle, D. (1996). *Visual tools for constructing knowledge.* Alexandria, VA: Association for Supervision and Curriculum Development.

Izard, C. E. (1992). Basic emotions, relations among emotions, and emotion-cognition relations. *Psychological Review, 99,* 561–565.

Izard, C. E., Kagan, J., & Zajonc, R. B. (Eds.). (1984). *Emotions, cognition, and behavior.* New York: Cambridge University Press.

Izumi, L. T., & Evers, W. M. (Eds.). (2002). *Teacher quality.* San Francisco: Pacific Research Institute.

Jackson, D. N., Ahmed, S. A., & Heapy, N. A. (1976). Is achievement a unitary construct? *Journal of Research in Personality, 10,* 1–21.

Jensen, E. (1995). *Superteaching: Success strategies that bring out the best in both you and your students.* Del Mar, CA: Turning Point.

Jensen, E. (1998). *Teaching with the brain in mind.* Alexandria, VA: Association for Supervision and Curriculum Development.

Jewett, J., & Katzev, A. (1993). *School-based early childhood centers: Secrets of success from early innovators.* Portland, OR: Child, Family, and Community Program, Northwest Regional Educational Laboratory.

Johnson-Laird, P. N., & Oatley, K. (1992). Basic emotions, rationality, and folk theory. *Cognition and Emotion, 6,* 201–223.

Jones, B., Valdez, G., Nowakowski, J., & Rasmussen, C. (1995). Table 1: Indicators of engaged learning. In *Plugging In: Choosing and Using Educational Technology.* Naperville, IL: North Central Regional Educational Laboratory. Retrieved October 7, 2003 from http://www.ncrel.org/sdrs/edtalk/toc.htm.

Jones, B. F., Palincsar, A. S., Ogle, D. S., & Carr, E. G. (1987). *Strategic teaching and learning: Cognitive instruction in the content areas.* Alexandria, VA: Association for Supervision and Curriculum Development.

Jones, E. N., Ryan, K., & Bohlin, K. E. (1999). *Teachers as educators of character: Are the nation's schools of education coming up short?* Washington, DC; Boston, MA: Character Education Partnership; Boston University's Center for the Advancement of Ethics and Character.

Joyce, B. R., & Calhoun, E. F. (1996). *Creating learning experiences: The role of instructional theory and research.* Alexandria, VA: Association for Supervision and Curriculum Development.

Kavanaugh, D., & Bower, G. (1985). Mood and self-efficacy: Impact of job and sadness on perceived capabilities. *Cognitive Therapy and Research, 9,* 507–525.

Keefe, J. W. (1979). Learning style: An overview. In *Student learning styles: Diagnosing and prescribing programs* (pp. 1–17). Reston, VA: National Association of Secondary School Principals.

Keefe, J. W. (1987). *Learning style theory and practice.* Reston, VA: National Association of Secondary School Principals.

Keller, H. (2003). *The story of my life* (with supplementary accounts by A. Sullivan & J. A. Macy; edited by R. Shattuck with D. Herrmann). New York: Norton.

Kessler, R. (2000). *The soul of education: Helping students find connection, compassion, and character at school.* Alexandria, VA: Association for Supervision and Curriculum Development.

Kline, P. (1973). *New approaches in psychological measurement.* New York: Wiley.

Kline, P., & Cooper, C. (1984). A construct validation of the Objective-Analytic Test Battery (OATB). *Personality and Individual Differences, 5,* 323–337.

Kohl, H. (1991). *I won't learn from you!: The role of assent in learning.* Minneapolis: Milkweed.

Kohlberg, L., & Mayer, R. (1972). Development as the aim of education. *Harvard Educational Review, 42*(4), 449–496.

Kohn, A. (1993). *Punished by rewards: The trouble with gold stars, incentive plans, A's, praise, and other bribes.* Boston: Houghton Mifflin.

Kolb, D. A. (1984). *Experiential learning: Experience as the source of learning and development.* Englewood Cliffs, NJ: Prentice-Hall.

Kolbe, K. (1990). *The conative connection.* Reading, MA: Addison-Wesley.

Kostelnik, M. (1992). Myths associated with developmentally appropriate programs. *Young Children, 47*(40), 17–23.

Kozol, J. (1991). *Savage inequalities: Children in America's schools.* New York: Crown.

Kroeger, O., & Thuesen, J. (1988). *Type talk: The 16 personality types that determine how we live, love, and work.* New York: Dell.

Kuhl, J. (1981). Motivational and functional helplessness: The moderating effect of state versus action orientation. *Journal of Personality and Social Psychology, 40,* 155–170.

Kuhl, J. (1984). Volitional aspects of achievement motivation and learned helplessness: Toward a comprehensive theory of action control. In B. A. Maher (Ed.), *Progress in experimental personality research, Vol. 12* (pp. 99–170). New York: Academic.

Kuhl, J. (1987). Feeling versus being helpless: Metacognitive mediation of failure-induced performance deficits. In F. Weinert & R. Kluwe (Eds.), *Metacognition, motivation, and understanding* (pp. 217–235). Hillsdale, NJ: Lawrence Erlbaum Associates.

Kuhl, J., & Beckmann, J. (Eds.). (1985). Action control, From cognition to behavior. New York: Springer-Verlag.

Kuhl, J., & Beckmann, J. (Eds.). (1994). *Volition and personality: Action versus state orientation.* Seattle: Hogrefe and Huber.

Kuhl, J., & Kraska, K. (1989). Self-regulation and metamotivation: Computational mechanisms, development, and assessment. In R. Kanfer, P. L. Ackerman, & R. Cudeck (Eds.), *Abilities, motivation, and methodology* (pp. 343–374). Hillsdale, NJ: Lawrence Erlbaum.

Ladson-Billings, G. (1995). *The dreamkeepers: Successful teachers of African American children.* San Francisco: Jossey-Bass.

Lafer, S. (1997). Audience, elegance, and learning via the Internet. *Computers in the Schools, 13*(1–2), 89–97.

Lankes, V. D. (1996). *The bread and butter of the Internet: A primer and presentation packet for educators.* Syracuse, NY: ERIC Clearinghouse on Information Technology.

Lazarus, R. S. (1991). *Emotion and adaptation.* New York: Oxford University Press.

Lebow, D. G., & Wager, W. W. (1994). Authentic activity as a model for appropriate learning activity: Implications for emerging instructional technologies. *Canadian Journal of Educational Communication, 23,* 231–244.

LeDoux, J. (1996). *The emotional brain: The mysterious underpinnings of emotional life.* New York: Simon and Schuster.

Lehman, D. R., Krosnick, J. A., West, R. L., & Li, F. (1992). The focus of judgment effect: A question wording effect due to hypothesis confirmation bias. *Personality and Social Psychology Bulletin, 18,* 690–699.

Lens, W. (1983). *Achievement motivation, test anxiety, and academic achievement.* Leuven, Belgium: University of Leuven Psychological Reports.

Lens, W., & DeCruyenaere, M. (1991). Motivation and de-motivation in secondary education: Student characteristics. *Learning and Instruction, 1*(2), 145–159.

Leondari, A., Syngollitou, E., & Kiosseoglou, G. (1998). Academic achievement, motivation and future selves. *Educational Studies, 24*(2), 153–163.

Lepper, M. R. (1988). Motivational considerations in the study of instruction. *Cognition and Instruction, 5,* 289–310.

Lewis, C., Schaps, E., & Watson, M. (1995). Beyond the pendulum: Creating challenging and daring schools. *Phi Delta Kappan, 76*(7), 547–554.

Lieberman, A. (1995). Practices that support teacher development: Transforming conceptions of professional learning. *Phi Delta Kappan, 76*(8), 591–596.

Liebert, R., & Morris, L. (1967). Cognitive and emotional components of test anxiety: A distinction and some initial data. *Psychological Reports, 20,* 975–978.

Lispsitz, J. (1977). *Growing up forgotten: A review of research and programs concerning early adolescence: A report to the Ford Foundation.* Lexington, MA: Lexington Books.

Little, J. W. (1993). Teachers' professional development in a climate of educational reform. *Educational Evaluation and Policy Analysis, 15*(2), 129–151.

Lounsbury, J. H. (1996). Key characteristics of middle level schools. *ERIC Digest.* (ERIC Document Reproduction Service No. ED401050)

Lynn, R., Hampson, S. L., & Magee, M. (1983). Determinants of educational achievement at 16+: Intelligence, personality, home background, and school. *Personality and Individual Differences, 4,* 473–481.

Malloch, R. D. (1990). *Identification of underlying components of academic awareness.* Unpublished doctoral dissertation, University of Texas at Austin.

Malone, T. W., & Lepper, M. R. (1987). Making learning fun: A taxonomy of intrinsic motivations for learning. In R. E. Snow & M. J. Farr (Eds.), *Aptitude, learning and instruction: Vol. 3. Cognitive and affective process analysis* (pp. 223–253). Hillsdale, NJ: Lawrence Erlbaum.

Mandler, G., & Sarason, S. (1952). A study of anxiety and learning. *Journal of Abnormal and Social Psychology, 47,* 166–173.

Marton, F., Hounsell, D. J., & Entwistle, N. J. (Eds.). (1984). *The experience of learning.* Edinburgh: Scottish Academic Press.

Marton, F., & Saljo, R. (1976). On qualitative differences in learning: I—Outcome and process. *British Journal of Educational Psychology, 46,* 4–11.

Marzano, R. J. (2003). *What works in schools: Transforming research into action.* Alexandria, VA: Association for Supervision and Curriculum Development.

Maslow, A. H. (1987). *Motivation and personality* (3rd ed.). New York: Harper and Row.

McClelland, D. C. (1961). *The achieving society.* Princeton, NJ: Van Nostrand.

McClelland, D. C., Atkinson, J. W., Clark, R. A., & Lowell, E. L. (1953). *The achievement motive.* New York: Appleton-Century-Crofts.

McClelland, D. C., Koestner, R., & Weinberger, J. (1989). How do self-attributed and implicit motives differ? *Psychological Review, 96,* 690–702.

McCombs, B., & Whisler, J. (1989). The role of affective variables in autonomous learning. *Educational Psychologist, 24*(3), 277–306.

McKeachie, W. (1986). *Teaching tips* (8th ed.). Lexington, MA: Heath.

Means, B., & Olson, K. (1994). The link between technology and authentic learning. *Educational Leadership, 51*(7), 15–18.

Messick, S. (1989). Validity. In R. L. Linn (Ed.), *Educational measurement* (3rd ed.) (pp. 13–103). New York: American Council on Education: Macmillan.

Mevarech, Z. R., Silber, O., & Fine, D. (1991). Learning with computers in small groups: Cognitive and affective outcomes. *Journal of Educational Computing Research, 7*(2), 233–243.

Miller, A. (1991). Personality types, learning styles, and educational goals. *Educational Psychology, 11*(3–4), 217–238.

Miller, J. P. (2002). *Education and the soul: Toward a spiritual curriculum.* Albany: State University of New York.

Miller, R., Greene, B., Montalvo, G., Ravindran, B., & Nichols, J. (1996). Engagement in academic work: The role of learning goals, future consequences, pleasing others, and perceived ability. *Contemporary Educational Psychology, 21*(4), 388–422.

Mischel, W. (1973). Toward a cognitive social learning reconceptualization of personality. *Psychological Review, 80,* 252–283.

Mischel, W. (1996). From good intentions to willpower. In P. Gollwitzer & J. Bargh (Eds.), *The psychology of action* (pp. 197–218). New York: Guilford.

Mischel, W., & Shoda, Y. (1995). A cognitive-affective system theory of personality: Reconceptualizing situations, dispositions, dynamics, and invariance in personality structure. *Psychological Review, 102,* 246–268.

Moline, S. (1995). *I see what you mean: Children at work with visual information.* York, ME: Stenhouse Publishers.

Morris, H., & Snyder, R. A. (1978). Convergent validities of the Resultant Achievement Motivation Test and the Prestatie Motivatie Test with Ac and Ai scales of the CPI. *Educational and Psychological Measurement, 38,* 1151–1155.

Mueller, C., & Dweck, C. (1998). Praise for intelligence can undermine children's motivation and performance. *Journal of Personality and Social Psychology, 75*(1), 33–52.

Murray, H. A. (1938). *Explorations in personality.* Cambridge, MA: Harvard University.

Myers, I. B. (1980). *Gifts differing.* Palo Alto, CA: Consulting Psychologists.

Myers, I. B., & McCaulley, M. H. (1986). *Manual: A guide to the development and use of the Myers-Briggs type indicator* (2nd ed.). Palo Alto, CA: Consulting Psychologists.

National Council of Teachers of Mathematics. (1989). *Curriculum and evaluation standards for school mathematics.* Reston, VA: Author.

Naveh-Benjamin, M., McKeachie, W., & Lin, Y. G. (1987). Two types of test anxious students: Support for an information processing model. *Journal of Educational Psychology, 79,* 131–136.

Naveh-Benjamin, M., McKeachie, W., Lin, Y. G., & Tucker, D. G. (1986). Inferring students' cognitive structures and their development using the Ordered Tree Technique. *Journal of Educational Psychology, 78,* 130–140.

Nenniger, P. (1987). How stable is motivation by contents? In E. de Corte, H. Lodwijks, R. Parmentier, & P. Span (Eds.), *Learning and instruction: European research in an international context, Vol. 1* (pp. 159–179). London: Pergamon.

Nicholls, J. G., Cheung, P. C., Lauer, J., & Patashnick, M. (1989). Individual differences in academic motivation: Perceived ability, goals, beliefs, and values. *Learning and Individual Differences, 1,* 63–84.

Nicholls, J. G., & Dweck, C. S. (1979). *A definition of achievement motivation.* Unpublished manuscript, University of Illinois at Champaign-Urbana.

Nicholls, J. G., Patashnick, M., & Nolen, S. B. (1985). Adolescents' theories of education. *Journal of Educational Psychology, 77*(6), 683–692.

Nieto, S. (1994). Lessons from students on creating a chance to dream. *Harvard Educational Review, 64*(4), 392–426.

Nieto, S. (2003). What keeps teachers going? *Educational Leadership, 60*(8), 14–18.

Novick, R. (1996). *School-based early childhood centers: Challenges and possibilities.* Portland, OR: Northwest Regional Educational Laboratory.

Oatley, K., & Johnson-Laird, P. N. (1987). Towards a cognitive theory of emotions. *Cognition and Emotion, 1,* 29–50.

Ogle, D. (2000). Make it visual. In M. McLaughlin & M. Vogt (Eds.), *Creativity and innovation in content area teaching* (pp. 103–114). Norwood, MA: Christopher Gordon.

Oldfather, P. (1995). Commentary: What's needed to maintain and extend motivation for literacy in the middle grades? *Journal of Reading, 38*(6), 420–422.

Olsen, J. T. (1974). *Jackie Robinson: Pro ball's first Black star.* (Illustrated by H. Henriksen.) Mankato, MN: Creative Education.

Ormond, W. (2000). *Pacific megatrends in education* (PREL Briefing Paper). Honolulu, HI: Pacific Resources for Education and Learning. (ERIC Document Reproduction Service No. ED446360)

Palmer, P. J. (1998). *The courage to teach.* San Francisco: Jossey-Bass.

Panksepp, J. (1982). Toward a general psychobiological theory of emotions. *The Behavioral and Brain Sciences, 5,* 407–467.

Paris, S. G., & Winograd, P. (1990). How metacognition can promote academic learning and instruction. In B. F. Jones & I. Idol (Eds.), *Dimensions of thinking and cognitive instruction.* Hillsdale, NJ: Lawrence Erlbaum.

Pears, D. (Ed.). (1963). *Freedom and the will.* New York: St. Martin's Press.

Perkins, D. (1992). *Smart schools: From training memories to educating minds.* New York: Free Press.

Perrone, V. (Ed.). (1991). *Expanding student assessment.* Alexandria, VA: Association for Supervision and Curriculum Development.

Pert, C. B. (1997). *Molecules of emotion: Why you feel the way you feel.* New York: Scribner.

Peters, T. J., & Waterman, R. H. (1982). *In search of excellence: Lessons from America's best-run companies.* New York: Harper and Row.

Phillip, H. (1936). *An experimental study of the frustration of will—Acts and conation.* Cambridge, England: Cambridge University Press.

Piaget, J. (1929). *The child's conception of the world.* New York: Harcourt Brace.

Piaget, J. (1970). *The place of the sciences of man in the system of sciences.* New York: Harper and Row.

Piaget, J. (1972). *The psychology of intelligence.* Totowa, NJ: Littlefield, Adams.

Pintrich, P. R., McKeachie, W. J., Smith, D. A., Doljanac, R., Lin, Y. G., Naveh-Benjamin, M., Crooks, T., & Karabenick, S. (1988). *Motivated strategies for learning questionnaire.* Ann Arbor: University of Michigan, National Center for Research to Improve Postsecondary Teaching and Learning.

Piper, W. (1991). *The little engine that could* [from the original story by W. Piper; illustrated by C. Ong]. New York: Platt and Munk.

Prawat, R. (1985). Affective versus cognitive goal orientations in elementary teachers. *American Educational Research Journal, 22*(4), 587–604.

Prenzel, M. (1988, April). *Conditions for the persistence of interest.* Paper presented at the annual meeting of the American Educational Research Association, New Orleans, LA.

Pressley, M. (1987). *What is good strategy use and why is it hard to teach? An optimistic appraisal of the challenges associated with strategy instruction.* Paper presented at annual convention of American Educational Research Association, Washington, DC.

Pressley, M., Wood, E., Woloshyn, V., Martin, V., King, A., & Menke, D. (1992). Encouraging mindful use of prior knowledge: Attempting to construct explanatory answers facilities learning. *Educational Psychologist, 27*(winter), 1.

Proctor, R. W., & Dutta, A. (1995). *Skill acquisition and human performance.* Thousand Oaks, CA: Sage Publications.

Purkey, W. W. (1978). *Inviting school success: A self-concept approach to teaching and learning.* Belmont, CA: Wadsworth.

Purkey, W. W., & Novak, J. M. (1984). *Inviting school success: A self-concept approach to teaching and learning* (2nd ed.). Belmont, CA: Wadsworth.

Purkey, W. W., & Novak, J. M. (1986). *Inviting school success: A self-concept approach to teaching, learning, and democratic practice* (3rd ed.). Belmont, CA: Wadsworth.

Rafaeli-Mor, E., & Steinberg, J. (2002). Self-complexity and well-being: A review and research synthesis. *Personality and Social Psychology Review, 6,* 31–58.

Raffini, J. P. (1996). *150 ways to increase intrinsic motivation in the classroom.* Boston: Allyn and Bacon.

Rand, P., & Others. (1991). Negative motivation is half the story: Achievement motivation combines positive and negative motivation. *Scandinavian Journal of Educational Research, 35*(1), 13–30. (ERIC Document Reproduction Service No. EJ423891)

Ray, J. J. (1982). *Self-report measures of achievement motivation: A catalog.* New South Wales, Australia: University of New South Wales. (ERIC Document Reproduction Service No. ED237523)

Reber, A. S. (1993). *Implicit learning and tacit knowledge: An essay on the cognitive unconscious.* Oxford: Oxford University Press.

Reeves, D. (2000). *Accountability in action.* Denver, CO: Advanced Learning Press.

Reisenzein, R., & Schonpflug, W. (1992). Stumpf's cognitive-evaluative theory of emotion. *American Psychologist, 47,* 34–45.

Reitzug, U. C., & Burrello, L. C. (1995). How principals can build self-renewing schools. *Educational Leadership, 52*(7), 48–50.

Richmond, V. (1990). Communication in the classroom: Power and motivation. *Communication Education, 39*(3), 181–195.

Riggs, E. G., & Gil-Garcia, A. (2001). *Helping middle and high school readers: Teaching and learning strategies across the curriculum.* Arlington, VA: Educational Research Service.

Robinson, J. P., Shaver, P. R., & Wrightsman, L. S. (1991). *Measures of personality and social psychological attitudes.* San Diego: Academic Press.

Rogers, T. B. (1973). Ratings of content as a means of assessing personality items. *Educational and Psychological Measurement, 33,* 845–858.

Rollett, B. A. (1987). Effort avoidance and learning. In E. de Corte, H. Lodewijks, & R. Parmentier (Eds.), *Learning and instruction: European research in an international context, Vol. 1* (pp. 147–157). Oxford: Pergamon.

Rosenthal, R., and Jacobson, L. (1968). *Pygmalion in the classroom: Teacher expectation and pupils' intellectual development.* New York: Holt, Rinehart, and Winston.

Ryan, K., & Bohlin, K. E. (1999). *Building character in schools: Practical ways to bring moral instruction to life.* San Francisco: Jossey-Bass.

Ryan, R. M., & Connell, J. P. (1989). Perceived locus of causality and internalization: Examining reasons for acting in two domains. *Journal of Personality and Social Psychology, 57,* 749–761.

Ryan, R. M., & Deci, E. L. (2000). Self-determination theory and the facilitation of intrinsic motivation, social development, and well-being. *American Psychologist, 55,* 68–78.

Salomon, G. (1981). *Communication and education: Social and psychological interactions.* Thousand Oaks, CA: Sage Publications.

Salomon, G. (1983). The differential investment of mental effort in learning from different sources. *Educational Psychologist, 18,* 42–50.

Salomon, G. (1984). Television is "easy" and print is "tough:" The differential investment of mental effort in learning as a function of perceptions and attributions. *Journal of Educational Psychology, 76,* 647–658.

Salomon, G. (1987, September). *Beyond skill and knowledge: The role of mindfulness in learning and transfer.* Address to the Second European Conference for Research on Learning and Instruction, Tubingen, Germany.

Salomon, G., & Leigh, T. (1984). Predispositions about learning from print and television. *Journal of Communcation, 20,* 119–135.

Sansone, C., & Harackiewicz, J. (1996). "I don't feel like it"; The function of self-interest in self-regulation. In L. Martin & A. Tesser (Eds.), *Striving and feeling: Interactions among goals, affect, and self regulation* (pp. 203–228). Mahwah, NJ: Lawrence Erlbaum Associates.

Scheidecker, D., & Freeman, W. (1999). *Bringing out the best in students: How legendary teachers motivate kids.* Thousand Oaks, CA: Corwin Press.

Schiefele, U. (1991). Interest, learning, and motivation. *Educational Psychologist, 26,* 299–323.

Schiefele, U., & Krapp, A. (1988, April). *The impact of interest on qualitative and structural indicators of knowledge.* Paper presented at the annual meeting of the American Educational Research Association, New Orleans, LA.

Schiefele, U., Krapp, A., & Winteler, A. (1988, April). *Conceptualization and measurement of interest.* Paper presented at the annual meeting of the American Educational Research Association, New Orleans, LA.

Schmeck, R. R. (Ed.). (1988). *Learning strategies and learning styles.* New York: Plenum.

Schmitt, A. P., & Crocker, L. (1981, April). *Improving performance on multiple choice tests.* Presentation at the annual meeting of the American Educational Research Association, Los Angeles, CA

Schmoker, M. (2001). *The results fieldbook: Practical strategies from dramatically improved schools.* Alexandria, VA: Association for Supervision and Curriculum Development.

Schoenbach, R., Greenleaf, C., Cziko, C., & Hurwitz, L. (1999). *Reading for understanding: A guide to improving reading in middle and high school classrooms.* San Francisco: Jossey-Bass; WestEd.

Schön, D. A. (1987). *Educating the reflective practitioner: Toward a new design for teaching and learning in the professions.* San Francisco: Jossey-Bass.

Schroeder, C. C. (1993). New students—New learning styles. *Change, 25*(4), 21–26.

Schultheiss, D. P. (2000). Emotional-social issues in the provision of career counseling. In D. A. Luzzo (Ed.), *Career counseling of college students: An empirical guide to strategies that work* (pp. 43–62). Washington, DC: American Psychological Association.

Secretary's Commission on Achieving Necessary Skills (SCANS). (1991). *What work requires of schools: A SCANS report for America 2000.* Washington, DC: Author.

Seligman, M. (1990). *Learned optimism.* New York: Alfred A. Knopf.

Seligman, M. (1995). *The optimistic child.* Boston: Houghton Mifflin.

Senge, P. M. (1990). *The fifth discipline: The art and practice of the learning organization.* New York: Doubleday.

Senge, P. M., et al. (1994). *The fifth discipline fieldbook: Strategies and tools for building a learning organization.* New York: Currency, Doubleday.

Shanahan, T., and Neuman, S. (1997). Literacy research that makes a difference. *Reading Research Quarterly, 32*(2), 202–210.

174   CONNECTING WITH STUDENTS' WILL TO SUCCEED

Shapiro, L. (1997). *How to raise a child with a high EQ: A parent's guide to emotional intelligence.* New York: HarperCollins.

Sieber, J. E., O'Neil, H. F., Jr., & Tobias, S. (Eds.). (1977). Anxiety, learning, and instruction. Hillsdale, NJ: Lawrence Erlbaum.

Silberman, M. (1996). *Active learning: 101 strategies to teach any subject.* Boston: Allyn and Bacon.

Sizer, T. R. (1984). *Horace's compromise: The dilemma of the American high school.* (The first report from a study of high schools, co-sponsored by the National Association of Secondary School Principals and the Commission on Educational Issues of the National Association of Independent Schools.) Boston: Houghton Mifflin.

Skinner, B. F. (1989). The origins of cognitive thought. *American Psychologist, 44,* 13–18.

Slavin, R. (2003). A reader's guide to scientifically based research. *Educational Leadership, 60*(5), 12–16.

Smith, C. P. (Ed.). (1992). *Motivation and personality: Handbook of thematic content analysis.* New York: Cambridge University Press.

Snow, R. E. (1977). Research on aptitude for learning: A progress report. In L. S. Shulman (Ed.), *Review of research in education, Vol. 4.* Itasca, IL: F. E. Peacock.

Snow, R. E. (1980). Aptitude processes. In R. E. Snow, P. A. Federico, & W. E. Montague (Eds.), *Aptitude learning and instruction, Vol. 1. Cognitive process analyses of aptitude* (pp. 27–64). Hillsdale, NJ: Lawrence Erlbaum Associates.

Snow, R. E. (1989a). Cognitive-conative aptitude interactions in learning. In R. Kanfer, P. L. Ackerman, & R. Cudeck (Eds.), *Abilities, motivation, and methodology* (pp. 435–474). Hillsdale, NJ: Lawrence Erlbaum Associates.

Snow, R. E. (1989b). Toward assessment of cognitive and conative structures in learning. *Educational Researcher, 118*(9), 8–14.

Snow, R. E. (1990). New approaches to cognitive and conative assessment in education. *International Journal of Educational Research, 14,* 455–473.

Snow, R. E. (1992). Aptitude theory: Yesterday, today, and tomorrow. *Educational Psychologist, 27,* 5–32.

Snow, R. E., Como, L., & Jackson III, D. N. (1996). Individual differences in affective and conative functions. In D. C. Berliner & R. C. Calfee (Eds.), *Handbook of educational psychology* (pp. 243–310). New York: Macmillan.

Snow, R. E., & Farr, M. J. (1987). Cognitive-conative-affective processes in aptitude, learning, and instruction: An introduction. In R. E. Snow & M. J. Farr (Eds.), *Aptitude, learning, and instruction: Vol. 3. Conative and affective process analyses* (pp. 1–8), Hillsdale, NJ: Lawrence Erlbaum Associates.

Snow, R. E., & Jackson III, D. N. (1992). *Assessment of conative constructs for educational research and evaluation: A catalogue* (CSE Tech. Rep. No. 354). Los Angeles: University of California, National Center for Research on Evaluation, Standards, and Student Testing.

Software Publishers Association. (1998). Report on the effectiveness of technology in schools, 1990–1997: Executive summary. *Technology Connection, 5*(3), 25–27. (ERIC Document Reproduction Service No. EJ566614)

Solomon, R. (1980). The opponent-process theory of acquired motivation: The costs of pleasure and the benefits of pain. *American Psychologist, 8,* 691–712.

Sorenson, S. (1991). *Encouraging Writing Achievement: Writing Across the Curriculum.* (ERIC Document Reproduction Service No. ED 327879)

Spangle, W. D. (1992). Validity of questionnaire and TAT measures of need for achievement: Two meta-analyses. *Psychological Bulletin, 112,* 140–154.

Spence, J. T., & Helmreich, R. L. (1983). Achievement related motives and behavior. In J. T. Spence (Ed.), *Achievement and achievement motives: Psychological and sociological approaches* (pp. 7–68). San Francisco: W. H. Freeman.

Spielberger, C. D. (1980). *Test anxiety inventory, Preliminary professional manual.* Palo Alto, CA: Consulting Psychologists.

Stein, N. L., & Oatley, K. (1992). Basic emotions: Theory and measurement. *Cognition and Emotion, 6,* 161–168.

Strelau, J. (1983). *Temperament, personality, activity.* New York: Academic.

Students say: What makes a good teacher? (1997). *Schools in the Middle, 6*(5), 15–17.

Sykes, G. (1996). Reform *of* and *as* professional development. *Phi Delta Kappan, 77*(7), 464–467.

Tallon, A. (1997). *Head and heart: Affection, cognition, volition as triune consciousness.* New York: Fordham University.

Tiberius, R. (1986). Metaphors underlying the improvement of teaching and learning. *British Journal of Educational Technology, 17*(2), 144–146.

Tobias, S. (1985). Test anxiety: Interference, defective skills, and cognitive capacity. *Educational Psychologist, 20,* 135–142.

Tomkins, S. S. (1984). Affect theory. In K. P. Scherer & P. Ekman (Eds.), *Approaches to emotion* (pp. 163–195). Hillsdale, NJ: Lawrence Erlbaum.

Toms-Bronowski, J. (1983). *An investigation of the effectiveness of selected vocabulary teaching strategies with intermediate grade level children.* Madison, WI: Dissertation Abstracts International.

Urdan, T., & Maehr, M. (1995). Beyond a two-goal theory of motivation and achievement: A case for social goals. *Review of Educational Research, 65*(3), 213–243.

Vygotsky, I. (1978). Interaction between learning and development. In M. Cole, V. John-Steiner, S. Scribner, & E. Souberman. (Eds.), *Mind in society: The development of higher psychological process* (pp. 105–119). Cambridge, MA: Harvard University Press.

Wadsworth, W. C. (1995). *Once upon a time tales: How the sea became salt.* NY: Barnes & Noble, Inc.

Waitley, D. (1996). *The new dynamics of goal setting: Flextactics for a fast-changing world.* New York: William Morrow.

Walsh, W. B., & Betz, N. E. (1990). *Tests and assessment* (2nd ed.). Englewood Cliffs, NJ: Prentice Hall.

Walsh, W. B., & Osipow, S. H. (1995). Personal adjustment: Career counseling and psychotherapy. In W. B. Walsh & S. H. Osipow (Eds.), *Handbook of vocational psychology: Theory, research, and practice* (2nd ed.) (pp. 295–329). Mahwah, NJ: Lawrence Erlbaum Associates.

Warr, P., Cook, J., & Wall, T. (1979). Scales for the measurement of some work attitudes and aspects of psychological well-being. *Journal of Occupational Psychology, 52,* 129–148.

Warren, R. (1997). Engaging students in active learning. *About Campus, 2*(1),16–20.

Webster's Third New International Dictionary (Unabridged, 3rd ed.). (2002). Conation. Springfield, MA: Merriam-Webster.

Weiner, B. (1986). *An attribution theory of motivation and emotion.* New York: Springer-Verlag.

Weinstein, C. W., Goetz, E. T., & Alexander, P. A. (Eds.). (1988). *Learning and study strategies: Issues in assessment, instruction and evaluation.* San Diego, CA: Academic Press.

Weinstein, M. S. (1969). Achievement motivation and risk preference. *Journal of Personality and School Psychology, 13,* 153–172.

Wenger, E. (1998). *Communities of practice: Learning, meaning, and identity.* New York: Cambridge University Press.

Wenglinsky, H. (2002). How schools matter: The link between teacher classroom practices and student academic performance. *Education Policy Analysis Archives, 10*(12). Retrieved October 7, 2003 from http://epaa.asu.edu/epaa/v10n12/.

Wentzel, K. R. (1993). Motivation and achievement in early adolescence: The role of multiple classroom goals. *Journal of Early Adolescence, 13*(1), 4–20.

Wepner, S. B. (1991, October–November). The effects of a computerized reading program on "at-risk" secondary students. Paper presented at the annual meeting of the College Reading Association, Crystal City, VA. (ERIC Document Reproduction Service No. ED340006)

White, R. W. (1959). Motivation reconsidered: The concept of competence. *Psychological Review, 66,* 297–333.

Wiggins, J. S. (1979). A psychological taxonomy of trait-descriptive terms: The interpersonal domain. *Journal of Personality and Social Psychology, 37,* 395–412.

Williams, L. V. (1986). *Teaching for the two-sided mind: A guide to right brain/left brain education.* New York: Simon and Schuster.

Wilson, S. M., Peterson, P. L., Ball, L., & Cohen, D. K. (1996). Learning by all. *Phi Delta Kappan, 77*(7), 468–470, 472, 474–476.

Wiseman, D. G., & Hunt, G. H. (2001). *Best practice in motivation and management in the classroom.* Springfield, IL: C. C. Thomas.

Wissick, C. (1996). Multimedia: Enhancing instruction for students with learning disabilities. *Journal of Learning Disabilities, 29,* 494–515.

Wohlsletter, P., & Briggs, K. L. (1994). The principal's role in school-based management. *Principal, 74*(2), 14, 16–17.

Wolfe, P. (2001). *Brain matters, Translating research into classroom practice.* Alexandria, VA: Association for Supervision and Curriculum Development.

Woods, D. R. (1994). *Problem-based learning: How to gain the most from PBL.* Waterdown, Ontario, Canada: Donald R. Woods.

Woodward, W. R. (1982). The "discovery" of social behaviorism and social learning theory, 1870–1980. *American Psychologist, 37,* 396–410.

Ziglar, Z. (1994). *Over the top: Moving from survival to stability, from stability to success, from success to significance.* Nashville, TN: Thomas Nelson.

Zuroff, D. C., Moskowitz, D. S., & Coté, S. (1999). Dependency, self-criticism, interpersonal behaviour and affect: Evolutionary perspectives. *British Journal of Clinical Psychology, 38,* 231–250.

Index